Praise for *Resenting God*

"John Snyder has written another must-read for Christians! If you're burdened by resentment, bitterness, and blame and want to live a positive life, you will want to read *Resenting God*. One of my favorite parts is, 'God is never less than we imagine him to be, but always more.' John shows this over and over in his writing with his unique way of really digging into a topic, discussing it, and talking it out with his readers. Resenting God is a down-to-earth and powerful book giving answers to questions we hear every day from people trapped in that cycle of resentment and blame. I highly recommend it!"
—*Gregg Bissonette*, Grammy Award–winning musician

"Every person should have a John Snyder in their life. Ideally, in person is best. Second best is in your vision, your ears, and in your heart. With his uncanny sense of the presence and to see and feel within, he gets to the truth. Yes, when things go bad, when things go wrong; when you feel or know that you can't control what's happening, you are upset. Angry. And who is there to blame? God is—He's let you down. Maybe again. Yet, he hasn't. In *Resenting God*, Dr. Snyder becomes your teacher, reminding you that God is in charge. Reminding you to trust Him to set the course and guide you through your healing journey, generating the necessary corrections. All you need to be is open, allowing Him to be your partner. Resenting God will become one of my annual reads, no matter what is going on in my life. Good or bad, it's a gift that will bring me present, deliver balance, and celebrate hope."
—*Judith Briles*, author of *When God Says NO*

"*Resenting God* explains in lay terms how Reformed theology and Object Relations psychology together inform how believers form an understanding of what God is like. It examines how people project human traits onto God and explores healthier ways to experience the reality of God in their lives."
—*Rev. Susan L. DeHoff*, PhD, author of *Psychosis or Mystical Religious Experience?*

"There is no panacea for the world's pain or the subsequent struggles, blame, and bitterness. However, Dr. Snyder has offered a potent dose

of truth and grace in an age where denial, resentment, and skepticism are becoming epidemic. This work is a balm for the struggling and an inoculation against lousy theology as well as one of its main symptoms: resentment."
—*Chris Dunn*, Piedmont International University, higher-ed.net

"Disappointments, physical pain and suffering, loss of a loved one; these are all things that chip away at our belief God is for us. Does He even notice us, our comings and goings? And if He does, then surely He is cruel when he allows suffering or refuses to heal my child's mental illness. John I. Snyder, in his wonderful transparent way, addresses each of our doubts in this book. With fresh conversations and examples, John encourages us to find our way back to a loving God and to allow His light to penetrate our darkest places, helping restore our faith though our trying circumstances remain. May we, too, cry out, as the father of the young sick child in Mark's Gospel (9:24) cried out in tears, 'Help my unbelief.' He is listening, and He cares."
—*Diana L. Flegal*, literary agent, freelance editor, mother of a mentally ill child

"Snyder presents a prevalent yet oft-unidentified malady that plagues unbelievers and believers alike—resentment. This disease begins wars; it wrecks families and insidiously creeps into our spirituality—namely, our belief in God. Steeped in a thoroughly Reformed, biblical faith and supported by historical and personal narrative, Dr. Snyder states an ironclad case for how bitter indignation is a symptom of a view of God rooted in faulty assumptions. We are hereby reminded that the most robust apologetic for the faith is the simple proclamation of the God in Scripture who loves us and intimately cares for the world. A thought-provoking, inspired read by a missionary who himself has faced trials and tribulations and yet lives in a humble, joyful poise toward God and neighbor. *Resenting God* not only describes an ailment, it meaningfully prescribes how to move toward the faith through habit and personal examination."
—*Rev. Dr. Henry J. Hansen*, Senior Pastor, Bidwell Presbyterian Church, Chico, CA

"John Snyder has identified clearly that resentment is contributing dramatically to the secularization of our society. God is not dead, but many focus their anger on the divine. Thankfully, John also identifies a cure and gives us hope for turning the tide and spawning a new Christian awakening. I commend *Resenting God* to all of our churches, colleagues, and friends."

—*Rev. Dr. Les Hyder*, Stated Clerk/Executive Presbyter, Presbytery of San Joaquin

"The unremitting pain we look upon in the world coexists with the Bible's insistence on God's unqualified goodness. One of those realities or the other will shape our conclusions about the very nature of God Himself. John Snyder is not a theoretician. He is a practitioner. Stricken early in life with a combination of physical debilities that made it difficult to walk and impossible to read, he was able to turn resentment aside and grow a confidence in the majestic perfections of God. This author means to convince us of the reasonableness of faith. He does not merely point the way. He leads us by the hand."

—*Ronnie Collier Stevens*, missionary pastor, Moscow, Russia

"Theologian and international pastor John Snyder writes as one who not only knows you very well but also knows a whole lot of other lost people too. What binds the reader to the author is the common experience of resentment and its children, blame and anger, as well as their good friend revenge. These are so common to the human experience that they are marked time and again in the Bible.

In *Resenting God*, Snyder provides a pastor's solid and thoughtful counsel for how any of us can embrace and experience repentance rather than resentment. His personal witness of resurrection reality on a Christmas day lost high in the Swiss Alps will bring a smile to the reader and prove fodder for redemptive thought for a long while.

This book explores thoughts and dilemmas familiar to thinking, feeling, and believing people. It is worth not just reading but discussing, praying over, and sharing for others' good. And for finding glory in God anew."

—*Rev. Dr. Paul G. Watermulder*, Board of Directors, *Presbyterian Outlook* magazine

"John Snyder draws on decades of pastoral experience to deliver a dead honest response to the deep valleys of Christian faith that almost every believer experiences at some point or another. Many books have been dedicated to offering encouragement for those hard moments, but what makes this one standout is Snyder's understanding of the anatomy of those low points. Rather than being content to simply describe frustration with God, Snyder does something bold; he pushes back on some common assumptions about how these faith low points come to be and offers mature, biblical, usable advice for believers who are ready to emerge from the valley into a new place in their faith. In *Resenting God*, Snyder strikes a beautiful balance between patient, pastoral understanding and wise, practical counsel in a way that will prove genuinely useful for readers."

—*Matt Whitman*, Pastor of Free Church in Lander, Wyoming; host of the podcasts *The Ten Minute Bible Hour*, *History Nugget*, and *No Dumb Questions*

JOHN I. SNYDER

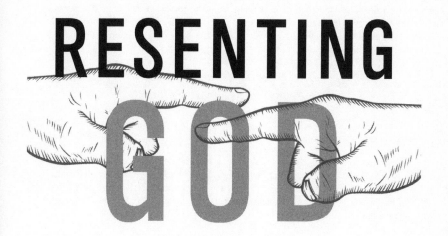

RESENTING GOD

ESCAPE THE DOWNWARD SPIRAL OF BLAME

ABINGDON PRESS
NASHVILLE

RESENTING GOD
ESCAPE THE DOWNWARD SPIRAL OF BLAME

Copyright © 2018 by John I. Snyder

All rights reserved.

Library of Congress Cataloging-in-Publication Data has been requested.

ISBN 978-1-5018-6966-2

18 19 20 21 22 23 24 25 26—10 9 8 7 6 5 4 3 2 1

MANUFACTURED IN THE UNITED STATES OF AMERICA

To my wife, Shirin,
with my deepest love and gratitude

CONTENTS

INTRODUCTION

Flashback to a few decades ago. It is Christmastime in Basel, Switzerland. The *Weihnachtsmarkt*, the Christmas market, has infused the town's social center with lights and color. Children, all bundled up, are dragging their parents through various little booths that sell specialty Christmas items. People are munching on *Chäschüechli* (a Swiss version of quiche), hot dogs, and a decadent cheese dish called *raclette*. (Who would have thought that boiled potatoes drizzled with cheese and spices could taste so good?) As I watched trams carefully weave through the pedestrians, I felt as though I had been dropped into a life-sized version of the miniature Christmas village at my parents' home, and I was reminded of the excitement of receiving my first electric train.

I have always loved Christmas. For me it is a time of joy and expectation. And as I was standing in Basel, with its Christmas market in full swing, things seemed brighter and more hope-filled than ever. Little did I know, however, that my world was about to crash in on me.

That Christmas I came face-to-face with a very different side of God—a more severe side—than I had seen before. But when I tried to express my grief, frustration, and severe confusion about my situation to my Christian friends and my pastor, I was told to praise God "just like Job did." Any honest or raw response on my part was discounted as unacceptable behavior for a "believer."

I thought I would never escape that dark valley of my life. Maybe you've been in a similar situation and have been told that it's bad form to admit to feelings of being let down by an almighty, powerful God. We aren't supposed to say that we're angry at him, even when we truly believe that he's directly involved in our grief. Why? Because it's just not proper, and of more concern, we'd be a "bad witness." We'll let Jesus down and others will be discouraged from the faith because of our failing witness. In fact, we may even be condemning others to hell, just because we couldn't muster up enough faith to trust God.

Have you ever been told that you shouldn't complain about God or feel any resentment or bitterness toward him? I'm here to tell you: that is a lie. I'll even go further and state an unpopular truth—sometimes we are actually taught to believe this lie. The pastor teaches us this lie. Church leaders teach us this lie. Even the larger institution of church teaches us this lie. I don't mean to fault or point fingers at the pastors and leaders who preach this lie, because I think they are probably living out the same lie that they've been taught—that we should lie about how we really feel, for Jesus's sake.

There's so much wrong with this thinking, and it does great damage to the reputation of the body of Christ as those who are called to be honest and trustworthy people. Yes, we may put on a bright smile on our grief and quote Job and the psalmists ad nauseam in church, but those on the outside looking in don't buy the false advertising. Why? Because it's not real.

Some of the most heartbreaking times in my life are when I encounter people who are obviously in a state of grief and anger but think they have to express the same clichés of "I'm just great with Jesus" to the pastor. They think that's what pastors want to hear and what good Christians do, and they don't want to disappoint. I want to tell them, "It's okay. I can see the rage in your eyes, your anger and disappointment in God. I've been there too. But I'm here to tell you that God has the widest of shoulders of anyone we know, and you being angry with him isn't going to bother him in the least. Neither is your being angry at God going to destroy someone else's faith or fail to lead someone to Jesus."

I'm here to tell you that God is bigger than our anger and our grief. Ours is a God who calls us into a relationship, one that is personal, real, and honest. And in any relationship, you're going to get angry, for one reason or another. How can we expect our relationship with God to be any different? Charles Spurgeon once wrote, "A man who has a strong mind can bear to be insulted long."[1] In other words, it takes a strong-minded person to take a long stream of insults. God is the only Being who doesn't take our tempers and rages personally. This can be hard for us to understand, because when someone attacks us (especially when we're innocent), our initial reaction is to respond in kind, and sometimes to totally destroy the offender! God is above all of this. The bigger person doesn't take revenge on someone who attacks him or her, and God is always the bigger person. So whatever we throw at him, however unpleasant or harsh or ill-advised it might be, he is not hurt or offended. He will not walk away from you. He can take it. In fact, he's the only One who can.

The greater danger to us, however, lies not in the anger we may feel against God as much as holding on to that anger. Sometimes you may feel it's impossible to let go, but anger, left unchecked, turns quickly to bitterness, blame, and deep-seated resentment, and this creates a destructive downward spiral. We *can* and we *must* get out of this spiral. Our spiritual life depends on it.

This book is about what to do when you feel resentment against God. Resentment can strike any person, anywhere, anytime, regardless of background, theological training (or lack of it), age, life experience, or level of intellect. It happens. But when you give in to these emotions, you can be pulled into bitterness and a guaranteed miserable life. The way out of this darkness into joy and hope is to acknowledge your sickness, look it straight in the eye, and then turn it over to the Great Physician, who can work his wonders.

I didn't write this book as a psychological cure-all for those suffering from anger, hate, or resentment. Rather, it is a place where I pray you can move out of the spiritually dark place you are in, to help you identify and work through your anger at God so that you can find restoration with the One who will walk with you and sustain you through any negativity in life, whatever may come.

Part One

The Causes and Consequences of Resentment

Chapter 1

WHEN ANGER TURNS UPWARD

It was an already-packed Saturday. I had a couple coming in for counseling, and I needed to attend a birthday party, was behind on my sermon preparation for Sunday, and was scheduled to do a funeral service, all on the same day. If there were no glitches, I would have just enough time to cover all my bases.

Everything seemed to be running smoothly at first. The couple left early, so I had a few extra minutes to prepare for the funeral service. From my window, I could see cars pulling up, so I went outside to meet the funeral party. With greetings exchanged, I escorted them back into our Fireside Room to go over the details of the service. I had half the party in one room, but the other half was somewhere else. I couldn't seem to get everyone together, so I pulled one of the pallbearers aside and asked him what the matter was. Apparently, there was a family squabble between two brothers, and they didn't want to be in the same room together.

Since we were already running late, I pulled one brother into the room and asked about the problem. He admitted that there had been a falling out between him and his brother some *forty years ago*. He couldn't remember what the cause was, but both brothers had managed to harbor their resentment against each other for all those many years. Not even their mother's death could pry apart the intense loathing.

This was nothing new to me. Whether officiating weddings or funerals, I find that there's usually some relative there who is angry with another relative. You might be surprised to know how many families will carry on a long-standing feud like this one, unwilling to mend fences and bury old grievances. Siblings, parents, ex-spouses, children—the list is endless.

Families, supposed safe havens for us, are often smoldering cauldrons of resentment and all that goes along with it. Deep-seated childhood envy is twisted into childish hostility. A simple family celebration can keep psychiatrists busy for months. Add to this the dynamics with in-laws and ex-spouses, and fallout from these times is a therapist's windfall.

Resentment seems to be multiplying and gaining a strong foothold worldwide, and not just among family members. If you search the Internet for "resentment," you'll find a wide variety of reasons why people are angry, envious, spiteful, or simply filled with the culmination of this disease: hatred.

Through years of pastoral counseling, I can attest that, if left unchecked, resentment is a powerful, deadly force. Just ask its victims. It is a cancer that destroys everything it touches. In seconds it can kill a deep relationship that has taken years or even decades to develop. It dissipates love, joy, and hope. It neutralizes marriages, churches, small businesses, large corporations, political parties, and governments. When it comes to Christian faith, it can eat up trust and confidence in God faster than a flesh-eating virus can dissolve the tissues of a human body.

Resentment can harm or delude you without your even knowing it. It clouds your reasoning, keeps you from recognizing the truth, and makes you incapable of seeing someone else's point of view. Bottom line: it hurts you more than the person you're resenting! And when you're resentful of someone, you can mistake your strong, heated feelings for logic. It's like trying to reason with a drunk person. You'd have to be just as drunk as that person to understand his or her logic.

Resentment, the great deluder, is often based upon a delusion of grandeur. The person harboring the resentment gets a false sense of power. In reality, this is just a short-lived burst of adrenaline. It is very similar to other addictions. You get charged up. You feel alive and good and then you need more. Just one more drink, one more smoke, one more X-rated film, one more pulse-raising fight. When those effects wear off, you're left in a far worse condition with lower self-worth, less self-control, and more self-doubt.

In a real sense, when you resent people, you put them in charge of your life. You end up the loser. Actress and novelist Carrie Fisher wrote, "Resentment is like drinking poison and waiting for the other person to die."[1]

What Is Resentment?

Resentment, envy, jealousy, bitterness, hatred, and similar emotions can lead to virtually any sort of physical or psychological disorder. Mental health professionals recognize this, so why do Christians often ignore or gloss over it? Resentment against God isn't typically discussed by church leaders or preached from our pulpits. Sure, we're aware of it among our unbelieving—or believing, but unchurched—friends. We even realize that many people's skepticism about God has stemmed initially from youthful resentment against him, leading ultimately to a full disbelief in his very existence. Today, however, there seems to be an increasing anger on the part of *believers* against God. We know what usually produces resentment against other people, but why against God—the One who claims to be our best and most reliable friend, the most loving and loyal being in the universe, the Creator of all things?

None of us is a stranger to this poisonous emotion, which manifests in so many different forms. At some point in our lives, we've experienced an aspect of it when we've been the victims of injustice, deception, abuse, and betrayal. Or when we felt mistreated and hurt. Or, if we're honest with ourselves, when we've permitted the green-eyed monster of jealousy to abide with us for a while. When in a group of believers, it's difficult to find those willing to admit that they could possibly be jealous or resentful of another's success or even that they resent another person.

Resentment of any kind isn't necessarily related to the *reality* of things; rather, it's often a response to what we *think* is real. It isn't difficult to see how a wide range of dangers can stem from this emotion. Most of us have heard news stories of people who seemingly snapped and went on to severely harm others. Or about an enraged employee who one day suddenly lost control and killed an office full of coworkers. News of heavily armed persons entering schools and murdering in cold blood is becoming more and more commonplace. Their motive? Often it's long-term, seething resentment against someone, anyone—parents, neighbors, or even God. The resentment is perhaps never addressed or confronted, but it is certainly ever present.

Time doesn't heal all wounds; sometimes they get much, much worse! Let's not forget that the first case of resentment recorded in history led to the first recorded case of murder (Genesis 4:1-8) or that resentment was one of the reasons that the religious leaders of Jesus's day demanded that he be crucified.

Why Do We Resent God?

God is the Creator of all things, the sovereign Ruler of the universe, the very embodiment of justice, holiness, and perfection. He's merciful and kind in all his ways and fair in everything he does. He should be loved and worshipped by everyone, everywhere, and always. You might think, *How is it even possible to resent him?*

After many counseling sessions with people who are angry with God, I've found the following to be among their reasons:

- I don't know who God really is.
- I struggle with God's sovereignty (he's in charge, and I'm not).
- I perceive some failure on God's part.
- Life's stresses are consuming me.
- I am having to face the depressing effects of aging.
- I struggle with unfulfilled promises.

- My life situation is distressing. It isn't what I expected.
- I fail to live up to my own personal expectations.
- I am discouraged.
- I have been mistreated and abused.

One psychology study found that even atheists (who claim not to believe in God) have admitted to being mad at God at one point in their lives.[2] I can't help but think that a leading cause of anger toward God stems from the ever-popular ice-cream-and-cotton-candy brand of Christianity being sold. Many of us were raised with this version of the gospel, reinforced every Sunday not only by the sermons but also by the songs we were taught to sing in church. Complete with a perky, finger-snapping tune, one song went like this: "Every day with Jesus is sweeter than the day before, / Every day with Jesus, I love Him more and more."[3]

How I wish that were true! Even though this song is beloved by many, it does contain some pretty dubious theology. It is difficult to find a single statement in the New Testament that encourages us to believe that every day with Jesus is sweeter than the day before. However sincere the composer's sentiments, it isn't a true reflection of normal Christian life. For most of us, this is just not the way it is.

Such ideas in these songs create a slaphappy, ever-euphoric model of faith that powerfully shapes peoples' expectations for a lifetime. If people are unable to detect reality from mere Christian advertising, the message gets garbled and they can feel completely betrayed by God. "I believed, but he didn't deliver," they might say. These unfulfilled "promises" turn their sweetness to bitterness against their Creator.

The frequent use of text messages today is a classic example of how we can misinterpret things. Relationships can be shaken or even end because texts are completely misunderstood. Even worse is the incomplete message. You get only half of it, think it's the entire message, and completely misconstrue the sender's motives. This can lead to broken trust and confidence in the person or a complete shutdown in communication, without even bothering to find out the true, intended meaning.

Similarly, when we don't understand what true faith is, we can't deal realistically with problems that arise in our lives. If we imagine that believers around us are living this kind of ever-smiling, always-cheery Christian life, then we'll be very hesitant to reveal any tremendous inner struggles we may be experiencing. Enormous battles with guilt, temptation, bitterness, or doubt will be swallowed or kept quiet for fear of not appearing to live the "victorious life." They may even seem unacceptable or forbidden topics within the faith community. Who wants to be known as the spiritual dwarf in the presence of all these giants for Jesus? Aren't we expected to trust God every minute and feel this enormous affection for Jesus all the time?

This false view places a further burden on those who, for some reason, find it hard to trust God or for whom things are getting worse each day, not better. I've known some saints who have brushed aside people's anger at God by encouraging them to chant catchy gospel songs, or they made matters worse by admonishing them, "Now, you shouldn't be feeling such things!" Let's face it—there are plenty of things in life we shouldn't be feeling or thinking, but we do anyway.

I can often spot resentment in someone's heart the moment he or she walks through my office door. Over the years, I've even watched close friends put distance between God and themselves. No matter how much you might try to convince them, they won't budge an inch. In their minds, God didn't deliver. They obeyed the rules, did the right things, but God didn't come through. Unless something happens to interrupt this line of reasoning, the believer ends up alienated and full of bitterness against the very One who is their most innocent and faithful friend.

Trying to get people to rid themselves of their resentment is often virtually impossible. They won't admit it, nor do they want to let go of it. I remember one leader of the women's group in our church who wouldn't give up her animosity toward "that woman" in the group. Sadly, the leader was diagnosed with terminal cancer and given just a few months to live. One day, I got a call from the hospital that she had to speak to me immediately. I rushed over. As I entered her room, I could tell she didn't have much longer on this earth. I approached her bed, and she feebly started to speak. In her last, labored breaths her final desire was for me to promise that "that woman" wouldn't take her place. Even in her dying hours, knowing she would be facing the great Judge, she couldn't let go of her resentment.

But it's not just about our friends or "those kinds" of church members. Whether we want to talk about it or not, admit it or not, at some point in our lives resentment against God can find its way into our heart. We can be sure that life will throw us many curves. At times we will find ourselves in the depths of despair, grief, or hopelessness. In a moment, all our securities and things we love may be snatched away, leading us to feel completely tricked by God. Unless we have a complete confidence that he wills our best, it will turn into resentment. Since he is totally sovereign and therefore holds complete control over our lives, we can easily come to blame him for permitting terrible things to happen.

Rejection of God's Sovereignty

Why did God permit it? This is probably the number one complaint that turns from a simple question into a smoldering rage against God and the Bible.

The Bible testifies to a principal doctrine of the faith—the sovereignty of God. He is in charge of all things and has enough power to do whatever he wants—at any time. This realization of God's all-powerful nature (his *omnipotence*) causes all kinds of problems for people when they try to reconcile this with all the horror and grief they see in the world around them or even in their own lives.

The common logic goes something like this: If God is all-powerful and holds sway over everything, everywhere, and at all times, and if he is all-loving and perfect in justice and fairness, then why does he allow the most terrible things to happen to me, my friends, my family, my neighbors, my village, my nation, and around the world? If he knows all things all the time without any exception, then he surely knows what's happening to me/us right now. In this case, he must be approving of it all. Or, if he isn't approving of it, then at least he's allowing it. In either case, although I'm praying day and night for some relief or escape from it, he must be saying, "I could help. I have all the power and resources to help, but I'm choosing not to."

It's hard to find an easy exit from this line of reasoning, but there are many ways people try to get around it.

There are philosophers—as well as ordinary church people—who argue that since God is all-loving and totally just in every way, he must not be all-powerful. He wants to help us, but he can't. As much as he would like to lend a hand, he's just not up to the task. This idea leads to a small, ineffectual God. There are others who insist that God is still evolving and hasn't yet reached the level of development where he's able to step in and fix things. So give him a break. Give him some time—a few million more years—to mature into full Godhood. This view of God, or a variation of it, is taken very seriously and is found even in some of our theological seminaries. But there isn't an iota of evidence for either of these lines of reasoning in the scriptures. To arrive at such a conclusion, we must toss out the Bible and its consistent presentation of God as the all-powerful, all-knowing, and all-loving Creator. The idea that God would like to help but can't—at least not at the moment—is no solution to our problem. In fact, it creates greater problems for us to solve later.

In order to protect God from blame, those who argue that bad things aren't really God's fault try another exit: Sure, he's all-powerful, all-knowing, and all-loving, but he has no connection with the evil things that occur. That's the devil's doing. If you've been diagnosed with cancer or lost your job, your mate, your child, or something or someone very dear to you, then God had nothing at all to do with it. He can fix things for you, normally at the end of time, but he wasn't anywhere around when the bad things happened.

As attractive as this option might appear to some, it still doesn't work. For example, let's try this analogy: A policeman is walking down the street and sees a man being mugged by three thugs. With his handgun, Taser, pepper spray, and police radio, he possesses all the power he needs to step in and rescue the innocent victim, but, for some reason, he chooses not to get involved and keeps on walking. He feels genuinely sorry for the man being mugged, and his heart goes out to him, but he doesn't bother to help. He might be in a hurry to get home, or perhaps he was tired after a long shift. For whatever reason, he takes a pass.

Is the police officer in any way involved and morally responsible? Can he be held accountable for his lack of action? Of course! We can't get him off the hook by saying that it wasn't his fault that the man was mugged. We can't say that he had nothing to do with it or argue that it wasn't his business. If he had the power to do something about it but didn't, then he was directly involved. We have every right to point the finger of blame at the negligent officer. It is much the same with respect to God. There's no exit route open to us by saying, "The devil did it!" If God is bigger than the devil, then he's in it up to the hilt.

Another big objection to God's sovereignty is the biblical claim that there's a God whose will and purposes are higher than ours, and who holds absolute authority or power over our lives in every way. The notion of an all-powerful, all-knowing God is inherently repugnant to many. They don't like authority, and they particularly don't like the idea of a Being—God or otherwise—who knows more or has more control than they do. It's always been that way. In the words of one young philosophy student, "I just can't relate to someone who's always right!" This young man couldn't (or wouldn't) accept the existence of a God who infringed upon his *own* sovereignty.

Let's be honest, by nature we don't like someone hanging over us telling us who we are, to whom we belong, and what we need to do. (Parents particularly understand this.) We don't like demands placed upon us by others. We don't want to live by someone else's rules or obey an outside authority. A God who has a will higher than ours is a God who gets in our way. We have plans. We have places to go, people to see, and things to do. A God who stands squarely in our pathway, claiming our time and occupations, who tells us that we and all we have and are belong to him entirely, is simply not welcome. He can be our audience, but not the scriptwriter or director of our play.

This resistance to God's authority was the original sin of Adam and Eve, who set their own norms and decided their own reality. They were the modern, up-to-date first parents of the human family. We, too, often reject the idea of divine sovereignty, which at first glance is so repugnant to human sensibilities. But as we'll explore later in the book, God's divine sovereignty is the greatest thing we could ever wish for.

God Let Me Down

Perhaps the most common source of our resentment toward the Creator is his failure to do what we have earnestly begged him to do.

"I pleaded with God for months to save my
child's life, but he didn't."
"I prayed fervently but still got a divorce."
"I asked God for the promotion, but he gave it to
someone else."
"I cried out to God for help, but my cancer is
spreading."
"We begged God to get us out of the hole, but he
didn't and we had to file for bankruptcy."

From the seasoned believer to the new convert, it's God's failure to rescue, heal, make happy, or do whatever we want him to do that triggers a process of progressive erosion of love for him. It is this perceived unwillingness and unresponsiveness on the part of God to hear our most ardent prayer that can lead to deep resentment and a loss of trust in him. Because God failed to save or give what was requested, trust turned into resentment, and resentment, left unattended, bloomed into full denial. This is one of the common roads to atheism. It is rarely, if ever, the product of too many philosophy classes or too much critical thinking.

It isn't at all uncommon for people to hold a grudge against God just for the way he created them. I know of a young man who was very successful as a youth pastor, but who suffered secretly on a daily basis because he was physically different from just about any of his peers. His body continually humiliated him. When he looked in the mirror, he was filled with disgust at what he saw. He deeply hated the way he looked. He reasoned that God knew, even before his birth, that he would be humiliated by such a body, that he would live under this curse while others were given spectacular, strong, and attractive frames to be proud of. He came to see God as some kind of ogre who took pleasure in creating freaks to be mocked and laughed at throughout life. The whole thing seemed grossly unfair and he felt it was God's fault. His unresolved resentment ripened over time into a full-blown hostility toward God, his departure from the church, and his open rejection of the faith.

Virtually any one of us could choose to walk down

this road. It's so easy to look into the mirror and see something we don't like—we're too tall, too short, too skinny or fat, with the wrong nose or ears, the wrong race or skin color, too much of one thing or not enough of another. This often develops into an obsession. We may arrive at that place where finally we ask, "Whose fault is this, anyway?" And then we hear a little voice whispering over our shoulder, "God did this to you!" Resentment begins to set in against God for making us in such a way.

Why, Lord?

Let's return for a moment to the illustration of the police officer and the mugging. If something bad happens to us, is God involved? Of course! Could he have stopped it if he'd wanted to? Yes. Is God right in the midst of both good and evil? Beyond a doubt! Again, the most natural question in the world, then, is: *How could a supposedly loving God permit my great pain, sorrow, self-loathing, and disappointment, or that of someone I care about?*

We live in the right here and the right now. We have created our own worlds, and for the most part our own lives fill up the entire screen. We resent God not so much for what's happening to our neighbor but for what just happened to us. We can find some pretty good reasons for our neighbor's problems (bad decisions, sloppy work habits, low morals, selfishness, his just deserts, pride, and so on), but we're astonished and highly offended that really bad things should come *our* way. Haven't you ever found yourself saying, "What have I done to deserve this?"

Perhaps you're thinking about something you have faced or are facing right now. You're doing an inventory of your own baggage. So let me spend a minute telling you about some of mine. I wouldn't want you to think that I've been immune to what you may be going through. I know too well what it means to resent God. I lived it.

In my late twenties, I underwent a major life change. From my early youth, my greatest love was sports and the outdoors. The only thing that got me through my years in school (I thought it was a prison for children) was either recess in the lower grades or organized sports in high school and college. I lived for vigorous physical activity and competition of any kind. It was my life. The only thing that took second place was watching films, reading, or just seeing the interesting sights around me. These great loves—sports, movies, and reading—were the things that sped me through life.

One night, at the age of twenty-eight, while playing intramural basketball to take a break from intensive study, I broke my knee. It didn't just break—it exploded. When I went down on the wooden floor, everyone in the gym heard the loud, sickening sound. Even before I hit the ground, I knew it was all over. I was certain that something so bad had just occurred that things would never be the same again. I was right. I was unable to walk normally for an entire year, and when I could finally walk without a limp or a cane, I could do little else. Rehab was out of the question.

After that night, there was no more basketball, no more running, volleyball, tennis, or anything of the kind. I could walk and do basic exercises, but nothing more. So it has been since. Today, I'm glad that I can walk. But at the time, in the prime of my young adulthood, when sports were so important to me, it was a terrible blow. God could have prevented it, but he allowed it to happen. What was the point?

However, I thought, all wasn't lost. Even though I terribly missed this great love in life, I could still see. I may have been only half of what I was before, but I was at least half! I could watch films, I could read, I could enjoy sightseeing and looking at the ocean, the beautiful mountains, the fields, and all the rest of creation.

The very next year after I broke my knee, I lost my ability to read. This took place during my first year of doctoral studies. It happened late one night, a few days after Christmas. As I was studying, suddenly a strange pain entered my eyes. At first I thought that I had just spent too long reading at one stretch. But the next morning, the pain was still there. I had no idea at the time, but this was the beginning of a rare convergence problem that by the spring would result in the complete loss of my reading ability. I was unable to read again for seven very long years.

This put me in a real dilemma. I believed that God had called me into the teaching ministry or the pastorate, yet he had taken away the one thing that a pastor or teacher needs most—the ability to read. Already I could do nothing except walk and do simple exercises, but now I couldn't focus on a printed page or even on objects for more than a few seconds. My general distance vision was good, but since my eyes were unable to converge normally, I couldn't hold an image and see anything for very long. I consulted every specialist I could find in Switzerland, New York, and California, but no one could help.

I was in the position of not being able to do any kind of work to make a living. Since I could still see, I couldn't be certified blind, and I wasn't eligible for any disability benefits. What does one do in a situation like this? I couldn't drive a truck or car, cook, sell shoes, dispense theater tickets at a booth, or even mop the floor. If I tried to read even for a minute, it caused such a severe headache and pain in my eyes that I would have to wait an hour or two with eyes completely closed before using them again.

In short, the two activities I loved most in life were snatched from me. At the age of thirty, I was facing life without a career and everything I valued. Talk about confusion and resentment—I lived them day and night. I wallowed in them. For years.

I can say without qualification that I was very much *unlike* the biblical character Job, who responded to his suffering by saying, "The LORD gave and the LORD has taken away; / may the name of the LORD be praised" (Job 1:21). And even though I didn't think or act much like Job, I did seem to have an abundance of Job's comforters around me, those three well-meaning people (Eliphaz, Bildad, and Zophar) referred to in my seminary days as Larry, Moe, and Curly (remember *The Three Stooges*?), who missed the point entirely and ended up making Job feel even worse. Also, like Job, there were always those around me ready to say things like, "Why don't you just curse God and die!" But the worst were those who said to me, "If you had more faith, this wouldn't be happening."

It took me years to square all this with a loving and caring God. But what I found was that God didn't lose his patience or his stubborn love for me. He withstood my anger and my questioning. I know now what I didn't know then—that God doesn't need our gifts and talents, our fine education, our intelligence, or our life service. He can accomplish anything he wants without us. What he strongly desires is our love and trust; what he values is our full abandonment to his purpose and will, even when nothing seems to make sense in our limited human reason.

Chapter 2

WHEN LIFE IS DISAPPOINTING

Have you ever felt that God made a promise to you that he didn't fulfill?

If it's true (and it is!) that God communicates with us, then there will be times when he appears to make a promise to you. It may be in the form of a scripture that comes alive, that jumps off the page while you're reading it. Most believers who have spent years reading the Bible regularly have had this experience. A verse, read dozens or even hundreds of times before, suddenly is so filled with meaning and so perfectly timed that it seems directly, supernaturally connected to what was being either thought or prayed about at the moment.

You pray, "Lord, I'm so tired. I'm being slandered and undermined at work. I need some kind of divine intervention just to keep my job!" No sooner had you prayed than you opened your Bible for your daily devotional and read these words:

> Do not fret because of those who are evil
>   or be envious of those who do wrong;

for like the grass they will soon wither,
　　like green plants they will soon die away.
　　　　　　　　　　(Psalm 37:1-2)

You continue to read the entire psalm, rejoicing in God's word to you. You expect that in just a matter of days, the entire problem will get sorted out and the guilty culprits will get justice in the most remarkable ways.

Or maybe you heard a sermon in which some word spoken struck home with such force that you just knew it came from God, that he was saying something directly to you. Perhaps the preacher quoted Proverbs 22:6 about raising a child in the way he should go and he will not depart from it. Or he quoted from Psalm 91:7,

A thousand may fall at your side,
　　ten thousand at your right hand,
　　　but it will not come near you.

But what if the "promise" you named and claimed and were absolutely sure God was making to you wasn't kept? You thought God was preserving you from disaster and disease, but instead you've been diagnosed with cancer. You thought that God was going to keep your child from straying, but you just returned from picking up your son at the police station. You felt tricked and abandoned. God led you to believe that he was near, but it seems there's no trace of him now, when you need him most.

I remember a conversation I overheard between a well-known spiritual leader and one of his colleagues. The leader was describing how his children were going haywire and that his life seemed to be out of control. The more he tried, the worse things got. His friend asked him if he had prayed about the problem, and this great spiritual guide responded: "Prayer doesn't work, you know."

How many times have you felt the same way? You've prayed earnestly for help or deliverance and ended up thinking that the whole thing was just an exercise in futility. Or you've been the victim of the ever-popular "health and wealth gospel." The preacher guaranteed that if you would pledge your money to his ministry, God would bless you richly. With seemingly total authority, he assured you that you'd be visited with unimagined prosperity and spectacular physical health. Willingly you gave him your money, but instead of those grand promises, you lost your business and the bank foreclosed on your home. Bankruptcy became your new friend. How did that affect your view of God?

Unfulfilled Promises

It happens. We believe with all our hearts that God has made us a promise or is going to do something we want and expect, yet it just doesn't pan out. In fact, not only does it not work out the way we hope, but the opposite happens! We are worse off than we were before, with a mistaken understanding of what a life of faith and obedience really means. Such crises of faith can completely undo years of spiritual growth. One of life's big disappointments can wipe out in a single weekend what a lifetime of gradual, steady faith has been building.

We needn't think of this occurrence as something new or that it is what happens only to those on the fringe of faith. Many of God's people before us have passed through periods of radical disillusionment with him. Such things are not uncommon among the most seasoned believers today and go as far back as the days of the Old Testament prophets.

Consider that both Jonah, a prophet with an ill temper, and two of the greatest saints—Elijah and Jeremiah—all experienced profound disappointment in their lives. Jonah fled from God because he resented God's mercy on his enemies (Jonah 3–4). Elijah was fed up with his calling and felt he couldn't go on another day (1 Kings 19:1-5). The powerful Old Testament prophet Jeremiah walked closer to God than most people of his day, yet he was so weary and disillusioned with the way things were going for him, so sick of the mistreatment and humiliation he was experiencing as a prophet, that at the lowest point in his life he accused God of lying (Jeremiah 20:7). Jeremiah was thinking the life of a prophet wasn't all it was cracked up to be. Life was much tougher than he ever imagined, and he wasn't sure God's assurances of protection (found in Jeremiah 1:4-8) were being fulfilled in the way he expected. In any case, it's probably not smart to call God a liar, but Jeremiah seems to have gotten away with it. As the old saying goes, "Prophets aren't perfect; they're only forgiven."

If you want to know how bad disillusionment can be, read Jeremiah's gut-wrenching words as he bitterly curses the day he was born:

> Cursed be the day I was born!
>> May the day my mother bore me not be
>> blessed!
> Cursed be the man who brought my father the
> news,
>> who made him very glad, saying,
>> "A child is born to you—a son!"
> May that man be like the towns
>> the LORD overthrew without pity.
> May he hear wailing in the morning,
>> a battle cry at noon.
> For he did not kill me in the womb,
>> with my mother as my grave,
>> her womb enlarged forever.
> Why did I ever come out of the womb
>> to see trouble and sorrow
>> and to end my days in shame?
>> (Jeremiah 20:14-18)

That's what I love about the Bible—it's brutally honest about all its characters, including God. It never pretends. It never tries to make us think that people or situations are anything other than what they are. It seems that much of our modern-day faith has forgotten this deeply and uncomfortably honest heritage of laying our raw emotions bare before God. "When did we forget our rich, raging heritage?" writes Paul J. Pastor. He continues:

> The Christian story is unflinching in its treatment of suffering. It looks the full horrors of the human experience in the eye—and refuses to turn away. It finds life and joy in the middle of it all. Our doctrine is rich with holy contradictions of blood and bandages, deaths and resurrections, and a hundred inexplicable moments of hope right when all seems lost. We have holy, angry, righteous indignation against the world's systems of abuse and oppression. And, of course, our spiritual ancestors often railed against God.[1]

What should get our attention here is that Jonah, Elijah, and Jeremiah, all three men of faith, called by God and sent out for extraordinary, supernatural ministry, reached the point where they prayed earnestly that God would let them die! If the prophets were brought so low in life, what makes us think that we would be immune?

Also, we need to remember that God did not leave

them in the valley of despair. That was only one chapter of their personal stories. The resolution to all three of their faith crises was realized only after waiting to see what God had prepared for them.

I Prayed for an Egg—and I Got a Scorpion

One of the most quoted promises of Jesus is that our heavenly Father is more willing to give us good things than even parents who dote on their children and wish to give them the things they want and need. Jesus said if our children ask us for bread, will we give them a stone? Or if they ask for an egg, will we give them a scorpion?

If my children asked for a piece of bread and I put a stone on each plate, they would probably say, "Okay, what's the joke? Very funny!" But if they asked for an egg and I placed a live scorpion in front of them, they would shout, "What kind of parent are you? That's crazy and cruel!"

But this is what some of us feel we've experienced with God, and it can have profound consequences. Let's face it—life doesn't always work out the way we expect. There may come a day when we pray for an egg and God appears to give us a scorpion, exactly what Jesus said would *not* happen (Luke 11:12). But if it looks like a scorpion, walks like a scorpion, and stings like a scorpion, then, in all honesty, what else can we call it?

If you think this has happened to you, it's essential that you get some reasonable explanation right away, or in time you'll take away from this a very false and destructive view of God. Here are some things you need to factor into your conclusion.

First, it's entirely possible that getting the egg you asked for is not that good for you, at least at this time. On the one hand, we tend to think that what we want at the moment is something definitely good and absolutely right for us. Yet how many times in life have you noticed that if God had given you what you asked for, it would have proven disastrous?

On the other hand, what appears at the moment to be a scorpion might turn out later to be the very thing that aligns us with God. The Bible is full of illustrations of this very thing. The Old Testament stories of Joseph, the Hebrews' exodus from Egypt, the lives of the prophets, and even the life, death, and resurrection of Jesus in the New Testament make the point clear.

Church history, as well as contemporary Christian experience, reenacts these stories too many times to count. From our family's experience in church planting, we could recount more than one instance when what we thought was a scorpion turned out in the end to be the breakthrough in the ministry we needed. In one sense, the scorpion *was* the egg we asked God for.

Second, only God knows what the egg looks like. The "good gifts" Jesus mentions are good for God as well as for us. The gift needs to be in line with his perfect will for us; if not, it isn't an egg, even if we imagine it is. So we need to trust God to define for us what is good and what isn't.

Third, the egg we prayed for may come only after the appearance of the scorpion. What I mean is that it is common for believers to pray and then to embark on a course of action only to encounter a scorpion standing in their way. If so, God allows it to be there in order to test our resolve in moving forward, providing a way around it or equipping us to defeat it. This pattern summarizes the entire history of his people. Remember, the life of faith is not intended to be merely a day at the beach. So the egg we very much want, and ask God for, might lie beyond the big, ugly thing blocking our way.

Finally, the saying of Jesus about the egg occurs in the context of prayer's *importunity*, the never-give-up attitude of coming repeatedly before God and lifting up our requests to him. The promise follows Jesus's admonition to ask, seek, and knock. The Greek grammar here is unmistakable: it means that we are to ask and keep on asking, seek and keep on seeking, knock and keep on knocking. The asking, seeking, knocking, and waiting transform us. They grow us.

If we were to paraphrase Jesus's promise about the egg and the scorpion, it would sound something like this: *If we pray for something good, God will not give us anything evil, harmful, or destructive.* He doesn't necessarily promise to give us *exactly* the thing we pray for, no matter how good it is; instead, he addresses the true need behind the desire. Whereas we live in a world of appearances, God lives in a world of absolute reality. How things appear at the moment may turn out to be quite different—even the opposite. Jesus warned us about judging merely on the basis of what things *seem* to be (John 7:24).

What we learn from these repeated experiences in the life of faith is that God is utterly and forever trustworthy, regardless of what seems to be happening to us. The only way we can come to this realization is to ride the wave all the way to the shore. The biblical point is made too many times to count: prayer and waiting, and more prayer and more waiting, go hand in hand.

It's the testimony of God's people for over four thousand years that God frequently gives us more than we ask for, or better than we expect. This truth is the oldest, longest-running witness. In God's appointed time, his gifts are on the lavish, overly generous side. So after we have prayed and waited longer than we planned, we can be certain that our Father will gift us with an overflowing basket of multi-colored Easter eggs. We can trust in his faithfulness.

When Our "Purpose" Fails Us

Questioning God's motives and actions (or nonaction) can eat us up. It's easy to develop a strong resentment against him simply by trying to live the kind of life we think he wants us to live. We try to accomplish something for the kingdom. We follow what we believe is his will for us, pray about his direction, get guidance from our mentors, and then fall far short in reaching our goal. We risk everything in carrying out what we think God has placed in our hearts to do, but in the end it turns out to be a total failure.

As far as we can perceive, we did no visible good and didn't advance the kingdom in the slightest measurable way. All that transpired was that we lost our investment and made ourselves look silly in the eyes of our friends and neighbors. Couldn't God have done something to head us off before we wiped out?

God has all power. He knows all things. He loves us and wants the best for us; the Bible and other believers affirm this to us. *Then why*, we think, *would he permit these utterly botched efforts and messy results in my life?*

This is what we sometimes see in missionaries' lives. Missionary history is full of testimonies to this. They launched out into hostile and unpredictable worlds firmly believing that God would provide and take care of them and guide them into a fruitful life and work. According to many of their testimonies, this often happens but not always.

I once knew a church member whose son spent years preparing himself in advanced linguistics to spend his life as a Bible translator. He labored among a remote mountain people whose language wasn't even written down. First, he learned their language by living with them for years, even before attempting to put it into writing. Ten arduous years later, he produced a copy of the Bible in this obscure language. But just weeks prior to its publication, the government outlawed the language. It was forbidden for anyone to use it any longer. The young man fell into despair and confusion and ended up taking his own life.

Consider also the life of William Whiting Borden, heir to the Borden fortune, who donated much of his wealth to missions. His years of undergraduate study at Yale University, and then three more at a Princeton Seminary, were wholly focused upon his envisioned future of becoming a missionary to the Muslims in China. While in seminary, I was excited to read about him in the book *Borden of Yale*, which was advertised as a "mission classic." I was expecting an adventurous read about the usual sea storms, dangerous excursions, miraculous rescues, and the like. But the surprising story went like this. After graduation, Borden was ordained in his denomination as a missionary, commissioned by the mission board, and set sail for China, but stopped off briefly in North Africa to study Arabic. Within a month of arriving in Egypt, the twenty-five-year-old contracted cerebral meningitis and died.

Died? I was deflated. This "mission classic" was depressing. As I put the book down, I couldn't help but wonder what kinds of questions must have crossed the minds of his parents and friends. What were his mother's thoughts after encouraging him to embrace the missionary life? Did God really call him to the mission field, and was it God's will for him to die in Africa at so young an age? Did Borden make a mistake in perceiving his calling and waste his life? These are not easy questions.

But no such doubts ever seemed to enter Borden's mind. The phrase "No Reserves, No Retreats, No Regrets" is attributed to him. He wrote "No reserves" in his Bible after being accused by his skeptical peers of throwing away his life as a missionary. He followed that with "No retreats" when he turned down several high-paying jobs, and he added "No regrets" shortly before his death. Twenty-five years old and, from his point of view, he had lived his life to the fullest extent and completed God's will for him.

Borden could easily have added in his Bible "No resentment," because he seems to have held in his heart the key to the problem addressed in this book.

Borden's seemingly tragic story is not rare. A great number of young men and women have entered the Christian ministry only to have their families brutalized, their mental or physical health broken, their reputations permanently ruined, their ministries terminated, and their faith deeply wounded. Faithful Christians have responded to God's call and ended up either in the divorce courts, financial ruin, or the mortuary. I know because I've met them. But even more stories along these same lines won't make the point any clearer: Things happen in this life that don't come with any easy or immediate answers. Resentment? There's plenty of it to go around, and for a number of understandable reasons.

During my many years as a pastor, I've witnessed people come to terms with the disappointment of their failed dreams and plans. I've seen hopefuls surge ahead with dreams of being great singers, actors, professors, or athletes, only to end up devastated when their dreams don't pan out. The truth is, we all have the tendency to get a bit shortsighted. We may falsely judge our strengths and abilities, set out to achieve our goals, fail miserably in the attempt, and end up years later in total disillusionment and frustration.

The good news is that it's often the failure of *our own plans* that proves to be our salvation. Only from the ashes of our destroyed dreams can we see, or even be open to seeing, the excellent role that has been written into the script for us by a higher, far more skilled Scriptwriter. When we realize that there is such a Scriptwriter and such a script has been written for us, we can save much wasted energy and heartbreak on futile efforts. Even if we're slow learners in this respect, or if we spend most of life off balance, we can still land on our feet if we pay attention to where he wants to lead us.

Life in the Fast Lane

The daily challenges of life can so easily lead to a frustration against God, for the simple reason that he allows them, and these struggles just don't seem to fit the way our Creator made us. Did you ever stop to think that our bodies, minds, and emotions are designed for paradise? Our sin nature entered through the primeval "Fall," Adam and Eve's first rebellion against God (Genesis 3:1-24), and the curse of it spread to every human being who followed (Romans 5:12). Yet, even this didn't completely erase our original design. We were created to live within an ever-renewing, healing, joy-filled, and rejuvenating environment of ongoing pleasure in the presence of God, our Creator and Healer. By virtue of the fact that God made us, we were outfitted for a stress-free, joy-filled world much different from what we have. Simply, it means that we were never fashioned or expected to live under constant stress, distress, fear, anxiety, guilt, and the like—the very things that mark too much of our daily lives.

We're not hardwired to carry around with us frequent and long-term guilt, anxieties about tomorrow, and the fears and dreads that press upon us on a routine basis. Guilt, for example, is supposed to last only a few seconds, like the warning light on a dashboard panel indicating that something is wrong. It should lead to instant confession and repentance of sin so that it can be immediately removed from us by the mercy and grace of our forgiving God. Unending guilt and long-term anxieties are foreign invaders and don't belong in us. Our original design is to live in a close, trusting relationship with our divine Caretaker, and if that's off in some way, we won't function as we're designed.

We can see more clearly how God created us when we observe how guilt, fear, anxiety, and grief cause our physical bodies to break down. Some emotions can renew and refresh us, while others age us and destroy us. We tend to wear lasting negative emotions on our faces and can't hide them from others for long.

For our imagined securities—money, property, health, social status, insurance plans, friends, and the like—we often work too hard and too fast, we walk too close to the edge, we keep impossible schedules, strive to achieve more, earn more, buy more, keep one step ahead of our neighbors and competitors, and so forth. Just because our society tells us that this is the way it's supposed to be doesn't mean that we're built to withstand the pressure or to survive the lives we've made for ourselves. However, no one ever ended up in the psychiatrist's office because of too much joy or a carefree, happy spirit. The one can literally kill us, whereas the other gives us life and health. Who says that we have to—or even can—live a high-anxiety life in the fast lane?

But the fact is that we do. For many of us, we feel that there's no way out of the fast lane. We're faced with the daily grind whether we like it or not, whether we agree with it or not. We have children to support, bills to pay, mortgages to meet, and appointments to keep. To stop is to die, or to end up on the welfare rolls.

Yet, you can't tear up nature by its roots, as the ancient theologians used to tell us. By this they meant that no matter how hard we try, we're still creations of God, designed for a certain way of life. There's no way we can alter that design or pretend that it's some other way, just because society tells us we can or should.

Jesus taught us to observe carefully how the other creatures around us live (see Matthew 6:26). Consider the birds. They get up very early in the morning and go about their daily business with seemingly great pleasure and interest. They search for food, which they usually find.

They sing their songs, build their nests, lay their eggs, and take care of their young with apparently minimal stress or distress. From all appearances, they are rather pleased with their existence. There appears to be no hanging of heads in chronic depression or mumbling about how unfair life is. We observe no suicides among them.

Think of the cows grazing in the field. They do what seems to us very boring work. They spend the entire day in the pastures, chewing their cud, lying around, and returning the next day to do the same thing all over again. Yet they seem perfectly content with their lot in life, and rarely do we find them running off in search of greater adventure or some other, more meaningful way of life. They lie in the shade together, rest in cooperation and unity, eat together, and together walk unhurriedly to their next destination.

Creatures of the natural world appear to live a life in perfect accord with their design. Their lifestyles suit them, and they are marvelously outfitted to their environment. But not with us humans! No matter what we do, we can't seem to find a way of life that fits us. In a life of frenzied and frantic activity and endless technology, we rush to work and rush home again (unless we're gridlocked in traffic), constantly check our emails and social media, text all the time, get sick too frequently, squabble and fuss, argue and struggle to get our way, and on it spins. One day, we're forced to look directly into the face of death and most are left to wonder what the point of it all was.

These daily confusions and distresses can lead to a very profound peevishness against everyone around us, including God who put us here. Specialists tell us that chronic stress (defined as lasting over three months) can alter brain chemistry to the extent that other disorders can develop in the sufferer and can even create serious distortions of perception as to what is real and true. This has an obvious and profound effect upon our view of God.

Sickness, death of loved ones, divorce, financial or job loss, depression—all such things aren't rare occurrences. They happen twenty-four hours a day, seven days a week. They happen just as often to church people as they do to those who haven't darkened the door of the church in decades. Unrelieved stress and distress leading to resentment can eat up faith and erode our trust in God by the simple reasoning that an almighty God could easily prevent such things from happening but chooses not to. Of course, we will wrestle with that, but God's up for the challenge. If we let him, he can transform even our biggest frustrations into opportunities to know him and understand him more deeply than we could imagine. Time is on our side here. As we wait, pray, and watch for

God's arrival, there will come a day and an hour when he turns our darkness into light and our despair into an overflowing hope (Romans 15:13).

Getting Older

The arrival of the first wrinkle marks the beginning of another inevitable fact of life—aging. It may seem odd to some that we'd come to resent God for the unavoidable process of aging, but it happens anyway. Instead of coveting the wisdom that should come with age, we value youth. We look in the mirror and see ourselves being transformed. We notice in our bodies the gradual loss of strength, abilities, looks, hair, energy, body mass, and all the rest, while arthritis, joint pain, fading memory, and all sorts of disturbing organ malfunctions and mental disintegrations join the party. Time (and gravity) slowly ravages our entire outward form, and our bones and muscles weaken. We slow down, get less agile, become out of breath more easily, eventually run out of energy and, finally, run out of time. Sounds grim, but it's true.

Who hasn't protested the insult of aging? None of us. Someone once described it as "being beaten up slowly, one square inch at a time." Each of us has our own ways of dealing with the inevitable. Some have embarked on a hot pursuit of the elusive fountain of youth, attempting to postpone the decaying process or slow it down by trying one new fad treatment or diet after another. Even Christians are joining the long parade of those who want to be forever young. We are daily bombarded with endless infomercials, commercials, and advertisements on how to combat aging. Some may even give us hope. But we get older whether we like it or not, and some of us manage to do a little better than others along this road. (One church member of mine played tennis virtually every day into his mid-nineties and still mopped up the young whippersnappers in their twenties!) But the day will come for each one of us when our bodies and our lives will fade and end—permanently.

There are only two ways of viewing this absolute, undeniable fact of aging and death. We can face it head-on and admit we're getting old, or we can go through all kinds of humorous gymnastics trying to postpone or live in denial of the inevitable. We might manage to have a thirty-year-old face, but the body we're dragging around betrays us. We can try to cream away all signs of aging, mask over it, or cover it up, but in the end it will have its way with us.

It's easy to see how aging and death can be a potential source of deep resentment against God. They are a slap in the face, an affront to our sense of independence and personal sovereignty. They mock the very idea of our being the masters of our fate. They stand as a very thick concrete wall in our headlong flight away from our Creator. We may sink into deep despair or hatred of our God when this process of degeneration strikes us or our loved ones. Or, more hopefully, we can find the happy road out of this trap that God in his friendly sovereignty has provided.

What's the solution? We'll talk more in depth about this later in the book, but I will say that God's solution to aging and death, those twin enemies of our intended solo flight through life, is so infinitely superior to anything that we could cook up for ourselves that only an all-powerful and all-merciful being could think of it.

When We Can't Seem to Get It Right

Another of the most common sources of resentment against God is the kind of discouragement that sets in after a long period of trying very hard to get better by our own efforts, only to realize that it's just not happening. Week after week, month after month, even year after year, some of us keep trying to follow the preacher's advice to lay aside that favorite sin, get more disciplined in Bible reading and prayer, improve our personalities or attitudes, get more holy, or overcome those addictions and chronic failings.

What we're sometimes led to believe is that if we'll just get ourselves to perform at a certain level of moral and spiritual maturity, then God will bless us lavishly, profoundly transform us, and lift our lives to a high plane of victory, prosperity, and joyful faith. The message is that with just a little more of our own efforts, we'll get better and closer to God as the days go by.

Instead, we often find ourselves slipping back into previous sins and weaknesses. We are distracted by the business and affairs of the world, and sometimes we wake up in the morning and wonder whether we're becoming greater saints or total unbelievers. You might even hear that voice over your shoulder that says, "God isn't really there," or, "Face it, he's not with you anymore." We're trying so hard, but long-held bitterness and anger toward others are still raging. Addictions are escalating. Our problems and temptations don't seem to be getting weaker, but rather they are gaining in momentum and strength. We sincerely want to become giving and forgiving persons, but all we can see are our ongoing weaknesses.

Living under this perfectionist teaching is similar to being a child unable to satisfy a demanding parent for whom nothing is ever good enough. Finally, in despair over attempting to be ideal, the defeated child turns in resentment toward the parent—the one who holds up the unattainable standard. Just like the discouraged youth who rebels against the tyrannical parent, a person unable to reach God's standards turns against him when God represents the unappeasable father or mother. The young person is sick of not measuring up and gives up in anger. "To hell with it all!" he shouts and walks out of the church, and maybe even out of the belief that a loving and fair God exists.

From his early youth, a friend of mine (I'll call him Charles) has never been able to please his father. Charles is much older now, and even though he's done everything he can possibly think of to make his father proud of him, nothing has ever worked. Nothing has been good enough. He has suffered his entire life with the absence of his father's love and blessing. Charles's father suffered from mistreatment by his own father, but instead of breaking the chain of this abuse, he simply passed it on to the next generation.

Amazingly, my friend managed not to transfer this hex on to his relationship with God (or to his own children), as so many do, but has been able to find in his Creator what he could never find in his father. But Charles is more the exception than the rule. In my counseling, I've run into many people who have allowed their view of God to be controlled by this negative kind of family experience. Far too often, how we perceive our parents (usually our father) will determine how we perceive God. The earthly father becomes the model of the heavenly Father, and this is often a formula for disaster.

Martin Luther labored for years in discouragement under the heavy burden of seeing God as an exalted version of a hard-to-please father. It was while pursuing an intense program of biblical study that he received the shock of his life; he discovered that the view of God he had held for his entire life was completely wrong. God was not the ogre he had thought. He was not the cold, unmovable taskmaster Luther had imagined him to be. Shedding his old bogus views, Luther walked into an ever-brightening light that allowed him to look back to his early life and see how he had been saddled with a profoundly twisted image of God.

Luther found that God knows very well that there's a huge gap between what he wants of us and what we are capable of doing on our own. God himself makes up the difference for us. In various ways, he "measures up" for us where we cannot. Let's keep in mind that if someone holds us to a standard of life that we can't possibly reach, then eventually we'll come to resent or maybe even hate that person. We will want nothing more than to rid ourselves of this tyrant. Far too often, we transfer this image onto God.

A variation of this same theme is the case of Jill. Jill has violated the laws of God so many times, and for so long a period, that she believes God could never forgive her. She thinks it would be useless even to hope for forgiveness. She assumes that no God in his right mind would or could cancel such a huge moral debt, so she concludes that she'll do whatever she wants and reap the consequences of her actions. Why not? There's no hope anyway.

The problem with this kind of reasoning is that since forgiveness is assumed to be too far out of reach, resentment against God increases for his being so impossible to please, and so unforgiving in nature. When we believe this, God can't win in either case, and we could not be more wrong about who he really is, as we'll discover.

Chapter 3

WHEN WE AREN'T SURE WHAT TO MAKE OF GOD—AND OTHER BELIEVERS

One of the most successful comedy teams in the history of film was Laurel and Hardy. Years later, they're still watched for their comical fumbling and bumbling. They elevated stupidity to an entirely new level. One of the trademarks of their humor was Oliver Hardy's chronic blaming of Stan Laurel for virtually every problem he faced. Whatever the predicament, he would say, "Now, here's another fine mess you've gotten me into!" Poor Laurel could never get credit for doing anything right, and Oliver was never responsible for doing anything wrong. Seemingly, some people have developed a sort of Laurel-and-Hardy relationship with God.

For ten years of my childhood, I lived across the street from the tenth tee of a golf course in California. I spent many hours gazing out of our huge picture window, amused by the antics of the thousands of golfers who passed by. Due to this favorite pastime, as well as serving as a caddie for golfers and looking for golf balls in the creeks and grassy areas, I probably have what could be equivalent to somewhere between a master's degree and a PhD in golfing behavior.

I've seen it all—the fistfights over who should have won the ten-cent bet at the last hole; the extraordinary degree of anger after a hook or slice; the cursing, spitting, blaming, and general buffoonery that accompanied the players as they worked their way around the eighteen-hole course. For a really bad shot, it was typically the fault of the grass, the tee, the ball, the club, the weather, the caddie, the position of the sun, or anything else.

Some players would get so enraged at a poor drive, they would hold both hands around the "throat" of the club, as if it was the neck of a goose, then lecture and curse it for its bad performance. On many occasions, the indignant golfer would vigorously toss the mutinous club high into the trees or into the lake after shouting, "Okay, *you* can go find the *blankety-blank* ball yourself!" The one thing I never witnessed on the golf links was someone who made a goofy mistake, beat his chest with both hands and shout, "I'm an uncoordinated, blaming, bad-tempered idiot!"

Blaming Others

Who among us fails to recognize, in our more honest moments, that universal failing of the human race to point the finger of blame at others? By our nature, we just don't want to be the ones at fault. Often, we try so hard not to accept responsibility for our folly that it even becomes amusing to those around us. We see *them* doing it all the time, but we rarely see *ourselves* guilty of the same thing.

Apparently, this is one of those highly unattractive characteristics we've inherited from our first parents. In Genesis 3:12-13, we read that when Adam and Eve were first tempted to go their own way and ignored the clear boundaries God had given, their first reaction was to try to lay the blame upon anyone other than themselves. Eve blamed the serpent. Adam blamed Eve. It appears that Adam even blamed God for giving him such an easily seducible wife! If there had been any others around to blame, no doubt it would have been laid at their door as well.

We are blamers from the word *go*. We blame and accuse anyone and everyone, even before it begins to dawn on us that we might share some milligram of fault for our problems. If something's successful, it's due to our ingenuity. If it's a big flop, we blame our subordinates for their ineptitude or underachievement. It's true on every level of life—marriage, daily work, politics, international relations, and the like. We blame and blame, and when in doubt, we blame some more. It is the one piece of infantile behavior we never outgrow. Theologians call it part of our "original sin." It means that by our nature we tend not only to disregard God and go our own way but also to blame everybody and everything around us for the sad consequences of insisting on our own will.

Have you noticed what a little child does when he trips on something and falls down? When you rush to help him up, he turns accusing eyes to you. You made him fall! It was your fault! We are no different when it comes to God and our problems. Who better to blame than the One who made us? We like to reason this way: God knew we would do something foolish. He is wise and powerful enough to have prevented it. He didn't. So he's the guilty party.

We accuse him for our difficulties and sorrows even when it's abundantly clear to all around us that they are the product of our own bad decisions. Our friends can see that we face problems caused directly by our own laziness, stubbornness, blindness, and self-will. Yet we always manage to find some new and creative way of viewing God as the main source of these failures. "Now, God, this is a fine mess you've gotten me into!"

When God Seems to Favor Others

Sometimes resentment toward God comes when we have strong ideas about what God is and is not obligated to do. For example, sometimes it seems that God is annoyingly generous toward those who we think deserve so much less. When this happens, we find gross unfairness not just in our lesser blessings but in the lavish blessings he grants to others.

Two New Testament examples come to mind. The first is Jesus's parable of the prodigal son, found in Luke 15:11-32. A man has two sons. The younger son wastes his inheritance, but when he returns home, he is warmly embraced by his father. The elder son, who had stayed home and remained diligent in his duty day after day, was furious and resentful.

It wasn't that the elder son had received a great deal less; it was just the fact that the younger, foolish son was treated so generously that irked him so much. This resentment at God's generosity toward others is understandable, but such resentment supposes that we can judge God's actions. It misses the point that God may have plans and purposes for other people that he doesn't bother, or need, to share with us.

The second story is found in Jesus's parable of the day laborers (Matthew 20:1-16). The employer promises a fair and generous amount to those who start work early in the morning, and he fulfills that promise to the letter. But in his generosity he decides to pay an equal amount to those who arrived later in the day. This kindness to those who don't deserve it really irritates those who think they deserve more than the latecomers. And why not? They worked harder, didn't they? In this parable, Jesus was speaking to those who were religiously self-righteous, who figured that God owed them a great deal more than the spiritual riffraff.

Like the prophet Jonah experienced, we don't like too much grace and generosity bestowed on those we dislike or on those who haven't been as religious or spiritual as we think we've been. In our fallen, sinful condition, we imagine that grace offered to us is not so amazing after all; it's almost as if we expect God to be gracious to us. But to others, whom we believe deserve considerably less, it's not only amazing but also profoundly exasperating to see such lavish grace. It seems so unfair. And the idea that God is unfair in this way can fester into resentment against him.

A False View of God

All of life's negative experiences—the disappointments and the losses, pains, and reversals—can and often do lead to a false view of God. If we are convinced by false teaching that God is the Santa Claus who exists only to bring us what we want, or that he wants peace and prosperity for us at all times, or if he is the kind of deity who turns a blind eye to our favorite sins and idols, then without a doubt we'll develop a theology that will lead us far astray.

What the majority of people think about God is wrong. This is true both inside and outside the church. By our nature we tend to imagine the kind of God we want—or imagine that there's no God at all—if it's convenient to do so. Unless our ideas are based upon his self-revelation, most of the things we conclude about God stemming from our own limited wisdom will cause us to think all kinds of erroneous things.

And this is exactly how the Bible describes it. In the writings of the Old Testament prophet Isaiah, for example, we're told:

> "For my thoughts are not your thoughts,
>   neither are your ways my ways,"
>   declares the LORD.
> "As the heavens are higher than the earth,
>   so are my ways higher than your ways
>   and my thoughts than your thoughts."
>   (Isaiah 55:8-9)

We hear the same from God in the psalms:

> These things you have done, and I have been
> silent;
>   you thought that I was one like yourself.

> But now I rebuke you and lay the charge before
> you.
>
> (Psalm 50:21 ESV)

Pastor and sixteenth-century reformer John Calvin called the human mind a factory of idols. He believed that we're in the business of manufacturing false views of God on a daily basis. Left to our own devices and imaginations, we invariably and inevitably create some image of God in our minds that has little to do with who he really is.

Sometimes our false view of God is shaped by those in a position of authority over us and leads to our resentment of him. For example, Tiffany was a highly religious woman who wanted her husband and children to be just like her. To that end, she prayed daily and did everything in her power to bring it about. One day, her daughter asked her if she could go to the biggest event of the year at her high school—the senior prom. Tiffany knew that there would be dancing there, an activity of which she highly disapproved. She told her daughter that she'd pray about it and ask God for his answer. A day or two later, she gave her daughter the anxiously awaited answer from God: "I asked God about the prom, darling. Unfortunately, he said no."

No doubt God does give us wisdom and direction when we ask for it. Often, he provides solutions to our most difficult dilemmas. He is not a God who remains silent when we need some word of encouragement or guidance. However, in reality, it's very likely that what Tiffany heard "from God" was just her own wishes masquerading as the divine word. All that she accomplished was to produce in her daughter a deep contempt and resentment toward God for being against anything that seemed fun. Whether dancing was right or wrong for her daughter, passing the buck off to God opened the door for her daughter to say in total frustration and disgust, "Both you and your God can get lost!"

Much of the preaching we hear today can give us a completely wrong idea of who God is and what he's like. We can end up disliking a being that is nonexistent. I remember years ago, every Sunday morning, being trapped into hearing this particular preacher ramble and rant. He would preach on and on, seemingly without end. His sermons had to last at least one hour, and sometimes two, if he got wound up. In nearly every sermon, he would pause, look upwards, and pray, "Lord, do you want me to stop now, or should I keep on going a little longer?" It was no surprise to his victims that God always said, "Keep going, Herb." Never, on a single occasion, did God ever tell him to sit down and give people a break. If you were a visitor to Herb's church, you might think that a God who couldn't tell good preaching from bad should be avoided!

When I am in counseling situations with church members, or even in conversations with nonbelievers, people tell me why they can't believe in the biblical God. When I ask them to describe the God they can't believe in, more often than not, their answer doesn't even come close to what we know of God. Following their response, I'm happy to tell them, "Well, the God you don't believe in has nothing to do with the God of the Bible. I don't believe in the God you described either."

Typically, this provides an opportunity to describe God in the way Scripture portrays him—the loving, generous Father. It's amazingly easy to focus on the wrong image when trying to put together an accurate portrait of who our Creator is. As I mentioned, we readily accept what someone else taught us to believe—our parents, pastors, aunts or uncles, friends, and so forth. It's often hard to shake loose what others have instilled in us for years.

Some philosophers of the past have seized upon this human weakness and exploited it. In the nineteenth century, German philosopher Ludwig Feuerbach persuaded most of Europe that the existence of God was nothing more than a projection of the mind. He claimed that what we think about God is just our own delusion. He believed we create a God of our own imagination, and then we project this fantasy upon the screen of the universe. This make-believe causes us to feel better about the world, Feuerbach argued. Without this illusory "teddy bear" or comfort blanket of our own making, we'd be unable to face the cold, cruel realities of the world.

Feuerbach's logic was not overwhelming. His views were wrong in at least one respect: it is just as easy to argue that the *nonexistence* of God could be regarded as a personal delusion, a projection of the mind by those who prefer that he not exist. But even though Feuerbach was basically wrong in his philosophical reasoning, in terms of real life and history, he was mostly right, after all. The Bible contains many forms of the message coming from God himself: "I'm not who you think I am. Stop creating gods of your own projection" (see, for example, Exodus 20:4; Leviticus 26:1; and Jeremiah 1:16). It appears that even God was in agreement with a few of Feuerbach's basic ideas! He complained that people were (and still are) forever substituting their own deities for the real thing. So we can at least thank Ludwig for describing things accurately on this one point.

If we want to rid ourselves of our resentment against God, we need to find out exactly who we're dealing with. Just as in normal human relationships, misperceiving someone's motives and intentions triggers much anger and distress when we don't take time to find out who they are and what makes them tick. Remember text messages gone bad? How much more important it is to know who God is and who he is not.

Our mistaken idea of God is the major obstacle we need to overcome in our journey out of our anger and bitterness. Whatever happened in our lives to bring us to this place of resentment against God doesn't really matter in the long run. The point is that whatever roads we took, whatever detours we made to get to where we are, there's a direct road back to our Creator. On our return journey back to him, we find some good news: joyful recovery, happy reconciliation, and full restoration await us. God doesn't want us to stay for long in exile, away from home. He waits with eagerness for us to come back. He'll run out to embrace us as enthusiastically as the loving parent longing for the return of the wayward child. Such a picture of the anxiously waiting God is given to us on the authority of Jesus himself (see Luke 15:11-32).

Christians Who Don't Act Like Christ

Having a false view of God often goes hand in hand with having a false view of Christians. The weakest, as well as the strongest, case for the truth of the Christian faith is found in the lives of those who call themselves Christians.

Some people manage to light up the sky as they pass through this life, while others just add to the grim darkness. In fact, many who call themselves followers of Jesus behave just like everyone else. It's often impossible to tell any difference. Skeptics love to cite such hypocritical behavior as justification for avoiding Jesus. By some odd twist of logic, this only furthers their resentment toward God.

It is just as often true that many have tossed out the gospel and the church simply because they've observed the depressing behavior of those who name his name, who talk the talk but don't walk the walk. How many times have we heard, "The church is full of hypocrites!" Ironically, God takes the heat for these Christians' failures.

This is such an important point. There is so much "fake faith" in our time, and there are so many who claim to be victims of it, that we need to get a few things straight.

First, when the real thing appears, it's difficult to deny or dismiss. For example, the nonprofit organization Open Doors lists North Korea as the "most oppressive place in the world for Christians."[1] Christians who are caught practicing their faith are arrested, horrendously tortured, imprisoned, and often put to death.[2] The North Korean labor factories produce some of the worst examples of concentration camp atrocities ever recorded, with accounts of the most horrific treatment imaginable. There are reports of Christians being crushed by steamrollers and used to test biological weapons or hung on a cross over a fire.[3] Because survival becomes the goal, it is the norm for people to blame others when things go wrong in the camp. But we are told that there are some people in the factories known for not blaming others—they're called Christians.[4]

In fact, these genuine believers accept the blame for the mistakes of their neighbors, thus taking upon themselves the torture or death of the guilty persons. It is in such ways that genuine faith comes alive for the many who know nothing of the Christians' Lord. There's nothing fake here. This is real Christianity at work. Wherever the Holy Spirit is present in the lives of people, such extraordinary things happen.

One of the new ideas Jesus introduced into the history of ethics is that of genuine goodness, rather than mere rule-keeping. Philosophers before him, such as Confucius, used "The Golden Rule": "Do not do to others what you do not want done to yourself."[5] But Jesus turned such thinking around by commanding affirmative actions. He said, "Do to others what you would have them do to you" (Matthew 7:12).

So we can see how Jesus consistently intensified the requirements of the law. He went beyond the mere following of rules and the blame game. He probed deeply into the human heart and demanded that by his empowerment we become the kind of people who want and seek the good. In witnessing the magnificent behavior of real believers, we can come to see images of the kingdom of God. It makes an enormous difference to witness Jesus's life illustrated in full color in the behavior of his followers.

Any Christian is probably used to this challenge: "If it's true that Jesus is the Son of God and only Savior of the world, and that he lives in his followers, then how do you explain the extremely hypocritical, intolerant, and malicious behavior of so many who call themselves Christians?" The Christian is sometimes forced to try to excuse away such embarrassing behavior. Consider the frequent use of that overworked but undernourished argument, "Well, Christians aren't perfect; they're just forgiven." But when put in that position, we can ask a few pointed questions that help the challenger arrive at some conclusions on their own.

When confronted by an unbeliever who questions the ugly and sinful behavior of church people (and we all can affirm that there is plenty of it), you could ask: "Do you think that these people are real Christians?" If the answer is no, then what's the problem? We're not talking about real Christians, anyway. Every group or society on earth has imposters within it.

If the answer is yes, then we could ask them to point to the exact teaching of Jesus they imagine the people are demonstrating and ask, "In what way is their deplorable behavior an example of what Jesus expected?" Rarely is anyone able to identify a single teaching of Jesus with which the bad behavior supposedly complies.

We've all heard the generic arguments before. "But what about the Crusades?" Similarly, the response is, "What teaching or command of Jesus were the Crusaders obeying? Can you point to anything Jesus taught that would justify this kind of behavior? Was it, 'Love your enemies and pray for those who persecute you'?" (Matthew 5:44).

. "But what about the barbarism of the Inquisition?" Again, "What command of Jesus were they obeying in carrying out these tortures? Was it 'Love your neighbor as yourself'?" (Matthew 22:36-40).

We could list numerous other examples that are heard every day: "What about hypocrisy or racism or arrogance or (fill in the blank)?" Christians are clearly defined in the New Testament as those who obey the teaching of their Lord, who have his spirit dwelling within them, and who give at least some visible indication that a change has occurred (or is occurring) in their lives. So those who blatantly and chronically disregard his clear commands and overtly disobey his word can't be called his disciples (John 8:31-32; 14:23-24; 1 John 2:3-6; 3:7-10).

It is valid, though cliché, when a Christian claims "not

to be perfect, only forgiven," yet this truth too often is used merely as a lame excuse for inexcusable behavior and for being indistinguishable from everyone else. Far better is this confession of the famous hymn-writer John Newton:

> I am not what I ought to be—ah, how imperfect and deficient! I am not what I wish to be—I abhor what is evil, and I would cleave to what is good! I am not what I hope to be—soon, soon shall I put off mortality, and with mortality all sin and imperfection. Yet, though I am not what I ought to be, nor what I wish to be, nor what I hope to be, I can truly say, I am not what I once was; a slave to sin and Satan; and I can heartily join with the apostle, and acknowledge, "By the grace of God I am what I am."[6]

If church people give no indication somewhere along the line that a profound transformation of life has occurred, we're under no obligation to think of them as Christians or to blame God for their bad behavior. Jesus said unequivocally that his followers would be known by their fruit. He made it clear that referring to him as Lord is of no worth whatsoever unless we are doing the will of his Father (Matthew 7:21). In the end, Jesus will say to those who never allowed him to be their Lord, "I never knew you. Away from me" (Matthew 7:23). Whereas it's true, as the New Testament tells us, that it's not the behavior that saves us; nevertheless, the behavior reveals the genuineness of the faith. It's the outward, observable evidence that the thing is real.

This doesn't mean that we're called to become the final judges of other people's eternal destinies. Only God can play that role. Even though we can't separate the sheep from the goats, we can and must distinguish sheep behavior from goat behavior (see Luke 6:43-45; 1 Corinthians 5:9-13). The believer who lapses into sin and, for a time, engages in evil or immoral behavior is eventually horrified by it. Later on, it even seems that it was a different person who committed the sins that were so offensive to their Lord. The Christian sins but doesn't continue to *dwell* in sin. He stumbles and falls off the path but has no intention of continuing along the road of evil. He's very ready to be forgiven and to get back on the pathway of light and life as quickly as possible. Even in a longer lapse, the believer is never comfortable in a sinful life. So whereas it's possible to be a weak Christian, a lapsed Christian, a stumbling and fumbling Christian who takes entirely too long to get into the groove, is it possible to be a wicked Christian? The biblical answer is an unequivocal no.

Happily, it's absolutely true that Jesus makes a difference in human life and in daily human behavior. It was true in the New Testament era and just as true in generations afterward. The celebrated *Letter to Diognetus* is an anonymous letter to an unknown citizen in the Roman Empire, dated in the second to third century. Listen to this description of the generally recognized quality of Christian life lasting far into the centuries following the lives of the apostles and original disciples:

> Every foreign land is their fatherland and yet for them every fatherland is a foreign land. They marry like everyone else and they beget children, but they do not cast out their offspring. They share their board with each other, but not their marriage bed. It is true that they are "in the flesh," but they do not live "according to the flesh." They busy themselves on earth, but their citizenship is in heaven. They obey the established laws, but in their own lives they go far beyond what the laws require. They love all men and by all men are persecuted....They are dishonored and in their very dishonor are glorified; they are defamed and are vindicated. They are reviled, and yet they bless; when they are affronted, they still pay due respect...and all the time those who hate them find it impossible to justify their enmity.[7]

It's amazing that such glorious life among Christians was still observable in the pagan world so long after the first apostles and believers had passed from the scene. The enormous power that had produced such spectacular behavior was continuing to be felt in later generations. When and where that power is present among believers today, such spiritual vitality will make an impression on the ever-curious world—a world entirely unable to reproduce or imitate it.

Chapter 4

RESENTMENT'S LEGACY

Resentment is never the end stage; it always advances. Like a pre-cancerous condition, if not dealt with properly, resentment moves into something even more malignant and injurious, manifesting itself in physical symptoms such as heart attacks, gastrointestinal disorders, drug addiction, alcoholism, and divorce, to name a few.

Resentment should never be taken lightly. It is an extremely serious matter that changes the course of human life in more ways than we can count.

The Politics of Resentment

Prison psychiatrist Theodore Dalrymple treated many patients who were unwilling to change, who had hardened themselves and were living with chronic resentment. He wrote:

Criminals are great resenters. Their skins are paper-thin where any harm done to them is concerned, but elephant-thick when it is a question of the harm they've done to others. When questioned, they at once resort to tales of wretched childhood, of violent and neglectful parents, and so forth. In an attempt to strip away their long-term illusions, Dalrymple asks them, "What is the actual connection between your hated father and the person you robbed?"[1]

Dalrymple concludes that resentment is not only blind but also blinding.

Even on a worldwide level it's easy to see the devastating effects of resentment turned into deep-seated and widespread bitterness. Recall your studies on twentieth-century history. What was one of the causes of World War II? Resentment! Following the close of World War I, some of the punitive measures built into the Treaty of Versailles led to such profound resentment on the part of the German nation that a powerful, overwhelming desire arose among the people to pay back the nations of Europe for what the Germans had suffered. It was paid back a thousandfold. Just one generation later, the world witnessed the bloodiest mechanized conflict of all time.

More history has been written by resentment than we could even begin to suppose. Dalrymple remarks:

Men who become dictators never forget the trivial slights experienced in their youth and avenge

themselves upon their former tormentors when they
achieve power. One of the first of the hundreds of
thousands of deaths for which the Ethiopian dictator
Mengistu was responsible was that of the man who
had refused him a scholarship to the United States.
The dictator of Equatorial Guinea, Macías Nguema,
who killed or drove into exile a third of his tiny country's population, was so uncertain of his own edu-
cational accomplishments that he took anyone who
wore glasses or possessed a page of printed matter as
an intellectual and had him killed. These examples
could, alas, be multiplied many times.[2]

The politics of resentment pop up in both poor and
prosperous countries. For generations, thinkers have
observed that those who have less than their neighbors
often develop bitter attitudes of envy and resentment
toward them. The subtle notion that "I deserve what you
have" easily creeps into our thinking and begins to undermine our foundation for ethics and morals. "If I can't
get it for myself, then the government or somebody else
should get it for me," or, "If you fail to give it to me, then
I'll be forced to take it from you." Such conclusions are
too quickly drawn and readily occur in the minds of individuals as well as in the parliaments of nations.

In the early part of the twentieth century, it was such
resentment that prepared the way for Marxism and Communism to sweep across much of the world, killing tens of

millions. Marxist philosophy teaches that history is determined by a bitter class struggle between rich and poor. When everything is reduced to this simplistic formula, the door is open for powerful forces of resentment to develop, and when it takes over or becomes institutionalized, its end is never good. The quality of human life and society will always plunge when this deadly emotion is allowed to develop into a political policy or a worldview.

The Bible teaches that the basic conflict in the world is not economic but is primarily between human beings and God, between our wills and God's will. It's *this* struggle that leads inevitably to the hateful feuds and selfish grabbing that occurs whenever someone has the opportunity to take from his neighbor. The Marxist revolutionary leader typically rushes to fill his own bank account first whenever he acquires enough power to do so. How often do we hear on the news that the dictator of some small, poverty-stricken country is discovered to have his own secret wealth?

Human resentment is never a small matter. The point can't be stated often enough. Ignoring resentment will lead to unintended consequences far beyond what we can imagine.

As damaging as our daily resentments against one another are, the consequences of our unresolved anger against God are far more destructive, not just for ourselves but for everyone with whom we come into contact. We can adversely affect someone's faith, shred their confidence and trust in God, and turn them against the One who has their best interest at heart.

A Contagious Loss of Faith

When my brother and I were very young, my parents felt that they needed to fulfill their parental duty and send us to church. So they stayed home while shipping us off to the nearby Sunday school. I remember plotting every Sunday about how we could sneak away from class. We soon became quite skilled in the art of escape. Before long, my parents discovered we weren't at Sunday school. They realized that since church evidently meant nothing to them, there was no reason why it should mean anything to us. So they started attending in order to keep us there. In this way, our whole family came to faith together.

You've probably noticed how common it is for people to pass on to the next generation their most cherished thoughts, feelings, and values. Liberals and conservatives alike often pass on their political views to their children. A Navy veteran often has sons or daughters in the Navy. A football coach frequently has a son on the local football team, and so forth.

Similarly, it's true that "faith is more caught than taught" and is easier to transmit by example than by a lecture. What children see their parents or grandparents doing affects their own values and behavior more than lectures on what they *should* believe or do. The opposite is also true. *Non-faith* is more caught than taught. Absence of faith, silence about it (expecting our children to "decide for themselves when they're ready"), or even hostility toward it is very easily transmitted. Children are great imitators. Those parents who display indifference or blatant resentment toward God or church will most likely pass along those convictions. What this means in a great many cases is that all the by-products of non-faith—the fruit of leaving God out of our lives—will be handed down as well.

We can predict fairly accurately what a life of non-faith can be like. We shouldn't be surprised to see alcoholism, drug and sexual addictions, violence, personal chaos, suicidal sons and daughters, bitterness, inability to forgive others, abuse, various emotional and mental problems, destructive behaviors, divorce, social maladjustments, and the list goes on. All of these problems will in turn contribute their harmful consequences to society in general.

All these results will rip families apart and prepare the next generation to pass along all the same things to their children. Generation after generation will hand over this baton as a curse until it's broken by the invasion and infusion of a life of faith. It takes only one break in the chain, one person in one generation, to change the sad course of a family's history.

The weighty responsibility of passing along the right ideas and values to the following generations is also evident in the modern education of philosophy and theology. When we track the lives of theologians, philosophers, and even Bible scholars who suffered from deep resentments against God, we notice that in each case, these men and women of faith moved from happy confidence in God to a bitter denial of him.

A biblical scholar I knew in seminary suffered to such an extent that he became one of his generation's most noted skeptics. He was so influential in the field of New Testament studies that thousands of young theological students were highly affected by his views. They went on to hand those skeptical views down to their students or parishioners. In this way, the faith of thousands worldwide was directly shaped by one man's personal and private resentments against the God who permitted him to suffer. So much of what today passes for serious theology, philosophy, or even science is in reality little more than simple autobiography, the fruit of one person's resentment—"I trusted God, but where was he when I really needed him?"

Atheism

Let's be clear what's being said here. Disbelief in God is too often merely a form of resentment against God. It may be open resentment of his failure to do what we want him to do, or it may stem from a more hidden resentment against his very existence and his authority over us. There are many who not only don't want God to be in their lives but also don't want him even to be at all.

From time to time, we run across someone who denies God's existence based on some intellectual question. But by and large, most were atheists by the time they were in their early to mid-teens—far too early in life for it to be considered the result of their mature reasoning. Generally, these are people who have *chosen* God out of existence. They resented him just because he was in the way.

So atheism (or agnosticism) is usually not so much a *conclusion* based on argument and evidence but rather a *decision*. Our inherited and deeply rooted "sin nature" keeps us from wanting God. Think about it. Ordinarily, we would be highly suspicious of a young person's final verdict on profoundly important issues such as human relationships, economics, politics, and the like reached at so young an age, long before any serious study and thought could be given to these issues. Yet this strange fact is hardly ever mentioned when the subject in question is God.

Atheism makes for an interesting study in human behavior. If someone honestly believes that there's no God, that should cause him or her simply to pity the poor, gullible dunces who believe in this illusion and to move on through life putting the whole thing aside. The matter would be considered completely irrelevant. Yet many atheists join organizations set up just for other atheists, subscribe to newsletters, create websites and billboards, organize marches, attend annual conferences, write books on the subject, try to influence legislation, speak on television, hold debates, and so forth. All this is done just to advance the notion that God doesn't exist. It appears as though God is extremely important to them, though—his nonexistence often seems to be the central focus of their lives.

The real problem of those who deny the existence of God is that their lives become full of contradictions because they go through their daily lives as though there actually was one. They still want to enjoy the fruit of a universe that has a God—that has meaning, purpose, reason, the existence of right and wrong, and everything else that makes life livable.

Atheism's aggressive and belligerent reaction to the idea of God's existence ("theophobia") looks, for some, very much like pretending that the object of one's disappointment or resentment is not there, something like a temper tantrum. It's similar to the kind of behavior we observe in the person who acts as though his or her abusive father or ex-spouse doesn't exist, or the parent who refuses to talk about the child who has gone astray and disgraced the family.

We need only examine the lives of admitted atheists to get some insight into the fascinating psychology of atheism. New York University psychology professor Paul Vitz summarizes some of the contributing factors to his early atheism:

- General Socialization (or It's Not Popular to Be Serious About Faith): Many are embarrassed by their religious background in a society that looks down on a high level of faith.
- Specific Socialization (or Faith Can Limit One's Career): It's often very difficult to be fully accepted into one's chosen field of work unless the faith of atheism is openly confessed or at least implied. Christian faith just isn't "in."
- Personal Convenience (or It's Easier Not to Believe): It's much more convenient to ignore the question of God than to face up to his existence. Freedom from sexual restrictions or ethical requirements, more time and money for oneself than for God or church, and the like

all play a role in the psychological basis for atheism.

Vitz adds that for many others, atheism stems from deep personal pain. Many people reject belief in God because of some traumatic personal experience in life. An abusive or absent father, loss of a loved one, ignorance of who God is or what genuine faith is, negative influence of shallow believers, even blatant ignorance of theological matters or the wholesale acceptance of some favorite scientists' atheistic theories, all contribute to the comfort of avoiding God.

A look at the early development of famous nonbelievers allows helpful insights into the desire not to have a sovereign God standing in the way. A study of Sigmund Freud, Ludwig Feuerbach, Diderot, Karl Marx, Baron d'Holbach, Bertrand Russell, Friedrich Nietzche, Jean Paul Sartre, Albert Camus, Carl Jung, C. E. M. Joad, Antony Flew, Mortimer Adler, and even Madalyn Murray O'Hair reveals many common features in the formation of their rejection of God. A leading factor in most of their histories is a father who was either absent or present but loveless or abusive. Resentment seemed to shift from the earthly father to the heavenly Father. (It should be noted that Joad, Flew, and Adler tossed aside their atheistic faith later in life.)[3]

I don't doubt that for some people there is a variety of factors in the development of their view of a world without God. But as the late philosopher Mortimer Adler suggested, these factors have more to do with the state of one's will than the state of one's mind.[4] Generally speaking, atheism, agnosticism, and skepticism are attractive so long as they are convenient. This is true not only of philosophical atheists but also of practical atheists, those who simply live as though there is no God. As many thinkers have observed, our intellects tend to follow our wills and emotions very closely. Consequently, our circumstances can alter things dramatically in just a short period of time. We all know the old saying, "there are no atheists in foxholes."

If all this were only a personal matter, if our resentments remained only a private concern, an issue of merely being a believer or nonbeliever, then it would not be so dangerous for society. But this is far from the case. A small handful of people who resent God, or even the idea of God, can undermine centuries-long positive influences of the gospel on society.

We live in a time when a single person can become so determined to change society that his or her social activism can lead to laws restricting the freedoms of many others, even large majorities who believe otherwise. In the last half-century or so in the United States, we've witnessed the abolition of Bible reading, prayer, and the display of the Ten Commandments in public places, the erosion of free speech of believers in the work place, and the removal of political or religious freedoms for many. Numerous court cases have stemmed from some students simply carrying a Bible to school. Christian literature has largely been banned from the marketplace of ideas.

Trying to persuade others to believe in Jesus and the God of the Bible is looked down upon. For many today, it's the height of bigotry and intolerance. The existence of Bible clubs for students is still looked upon with great suspicion by hostile parents and school administrators. The social and political consequences of all this for our nation have been immense. This was due primarily to the dedicated actions in the twentieth century of those who held firmly to the blind faith of atheism—more precisely, *atheistic fundamentalism.*

Philosophical atheism, of the sort we're familiar with today, is a relative newcomer in the history of ideas but has managed in a brief period of time to sideline the faith that served as the North Star of social and political life for many generations. It is the belief of a small minority who, in a fundamental misperception of the First Amendment, demand that God be omitted from all public life.[5]

Ignorance of Religions

The ripple effect of personal antagonism and resentment toward a personal, sovereign God spreads ever wider, resulting in a massive, society-wide ignorance regarding Christian faith. This is now evident in the grotesque misrepresentations of it in the media. It is difficult to find anyone in media today, including news, films, late-night TV, and so forth, who can give even a simple account of the basics of the faith when covering a story involving the church, a pastor, or a religious issue.

This casual indifference to the complexities and subtleties of Christian theology spreads to the blurring of all faiths. Since the question of truth has been given up, it doesn't matter what the details are, so it's rare to find a commentator or reporter who is conversant in the rudiments of any of the world's principal religions. For the vast majority of people in North America or Europe, any religion is just about the same as any other. They're viewed as fairly similar to one another, trying to get at the same things, having the same values, and more or less worshipping the same God. Any squabbles between them are seen to be innocuous and irrelevant, minor differences occurring within one great family of brothers and sisters. One god is as good (or bad) as any other.

It's imagined that time, more communication, and increased knowledge and interaction will eventually blur these minor differences as we all learn more about one another's beliefs and come to see that one world religion is the most natural outcome. This open-armed leveling of all religions—seen as the pinnacle of enlightened achievement—leads to a leveling of moralities and mores and, eventually, to a complete undermining of right and wrong, good and evil. Reason and common sense don't permit any other alternative. Right and wrong, truth and falsehood, good and evil, justice and injustice, the ideas of fair and unfair all vanish before our eyes.

Such basic things come as the fruit of our "religious" beliefs. What we think about God (or "the gods") will directly shape all our ideas. How we view private property, government, economics, law, crime, education, sexuality, and all the rest invariably flows from the fountain of religion. If we don't get that right, everything else will eventually unravel.

The Effects on Society

All these consequences—political conflicts, contagious loss of faith, atheism, and ignorance about religion—result from the resentments that spring up in the human heart against a personal, almighty, and all-knowing God. The tiny mustard seed of resentment will eventually grow and flourish into a huge tree of misperception of who this God is. And this misperception of life's most basic fact will always bear the poisonous fruit that kills those societies that eat of it.

This issue is too important to let it pass by. Before moving forward, recall some of your lessons from French history. Benjamin Franklin called France—one of his favorite countries—a nation of atheists. He loved the country and the people, but he also recognized the truth that the rejection of God was at the heart of its problems. The French people had been inspired by the success of the American Revolution in 1776 and, with that as their model, attempted one of their own in 1789. The difference between a revolution among believers in God and one among nonbelievers was abundantly and painfully evident.

The former ended up with the longest-lasting and most prosperous free society in world history. The latter got saddled with just another tyrant (Napoleon) in a long list of others. Following the revolution designed to produce "liberty, equality, and fraternity," a virtual forest of guillotines was erected all over France and the people witnessed one of their bloodiest periods of human carnage and folly. A number of different governments in France have come and gone since then. We cannot help wondering if the entire history of France could have been very different had not hundreds of thousands of committed Christians (the Huguenots) been expelled from the country a century before the revolution.

Consider also the great nation of Russia. In my view, its revolution and longing for freedom backfired because the Russian people turned away from God and toward Marxist philosophers. The tens of millions of brutal deaths, the prison camps, and the poverty, suffering, and squalor that resulted from the reign of Communism were the direct fruit of their resentment of the rule of God over all of life.

Contrast the combined histories of France and Russia, given to the fruit of rebellion and a deep resentment against an almighty God, with that of ancient Israel. This tiny community of people gathered together under the banner of God, the Creator and provider of all good things. They had little power, little military or economic strength, and nothing to commend them among the mighty nations of the ancient world. Yet they managed to survive, even thrive, among them. They defeated the most powerful armies known at the time, sometimes with only a handful of fighting men. They managed to acquire immense wealth, outlast even the great empires of their time, and flourish when others died out by internal weakness and rot.

Israel's one and only claim to fame was their God. In all Hebrew literature they pointed consistently to God alone as their one and only hope, their strength, and their reason for existence. When they stayed true to their God, they prospered and lived in freedom. When they forgot God and drifted into idolatry, both their freedom and their prosperity dried up.

It remains to be seen whether the freedom and prosperity of the past will continue as more and more of America seeks to remove God from its institutions and its social and moral life. The age-old signs of social decay are already the subject of sermons and debates by believers, as well as political pundits.

Resenting God, and thereby rejecting the gifts that come only from his presence, is the root that leads to innumerable other maladies, personal and social. We could go on and on, but by now you've heard enough. Like any messenger of the gospel, we should not dwell any longer than necessary on the bad news but get to the good news. For the good far outstrips the bad, and hope—biblical hope—far outweighs the hopelessness and despair that govern too many people's lives.

There is a medicine that works when applied undiluted. It comes from God, not from us. It works because it originates in the mind of the one who designed and built us, who knows everything there is to know about us. No substitutes will do.

Part Two

The Cure for Resentment

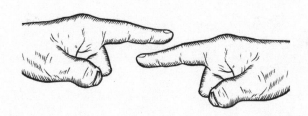

Chapter 5

A CORRECT VIEW OF GOD

As we've discussed at length, resentment against God is usually the result of our distorted or false views of him. But the good news is that it is possible to have a more accurate view of him and to learn to give him the adoration and love he deserves. To do this, it's essential for us not only to rediscover exactly who he is and what he wants for us, but also to return to a grateful trust relationship with him.

God is inviting us to take a deliberate step into his purpose, to become reacquainted with God the Father and Jesus the Son. He invites us to learn once again to place our entire confidence in him and to move away from resentment to a life of happy, God-glorifying fulfillment.

Understanding God's Purpose for Our Lives

God is so easily misunderstood. In fact, I'd say he's the most misunderstood being in the universe! God always and forever operates with a well-defined, unrelenting purpose that can often be misunderstood.

While in seminary, a friend of mine had an overarching, all-consuming purpose in life. He was determined to finish seminary at the top of his class and earn such excellent grades that he'd be admitted into what he considered the finest PhD program in the world, into which only a very small number of top candidates from across the globe were admitted each year. This is how he set out to do it. He turned his daily schedule upside down. When others were retiring for the night at 1:00 am, he would wake up, go for a run, and then begin his study. After three hours, he would run again, study until breakfast, eat, and go to class. After dinner he would immediately go to sleep and do it all over again.

Unbelievably committed, he kept this schedule for three years, removing every distraction from his life. It worked. He achieved his goal, but he was certainly not considered the life of the party, and he was completely misperceived by the other students. He possessed a great sense of humor and was gifted with an unusual brilliance, and to those who knew him and understood his plan, they found him very friendly, personable, and kind. But perceptions of him and his behavior were radically different from one person to another, depending on how they understood what he was trying to do.

Here's my point: we frequently misjudge those who possess a clear plan and act with an unwavering purpose. The stronger and more defined the purpose, and the more one is committed to it, the greater the mystery will be.

God is such a person. He acts every minute of every day according to a purpose and plan far transcending anything my friend had in mind. God is unrelenting and doesn't waver from it, even for an instant. It is so important to him that he doesn't give the slightest thought to whether we like it or not—our approval or disapproval hasn't the minutest effect upon his commitment to it. He is grieved when we misperceive his pure and good intentions and question his character or motives, but he never considers putting his plan aside to gain our approval or become popular enough to win our votes.

So what is his purpose? He is unflinchingly committed to our ultimate salvation. He acts behind the scenes in ways we can't begin to comprehend or appreciate. He speaks in ways we easily misinterpret and even disapprove of. He carries out plans that far exceed our ability to grasp, and he does so whether or not we are angry or resentful toward him. Sometimes all we can imagine is that he is cruel, loveless, capricious, indifferent, or even wicked. But he is the exact opposite! Generation after generation, he is the tender, loyal parent who willingly suffers all the rejection and accusations from the rebellious and foolish child, knowing that he has the beloved son or daughter in mind at all times (Luke 13:34; Luke 15:11-31; Romans 8:28).

When trying to understand the Creator of all things, we need to remember that he is absolutely sovereign. He is the King of heaven, Ruler of all, uncontested Master of all that is, and he has no equals in this world or any other. God is never surprised or dismayed by anything that comes to pass. He decrees what he wills and nothing occurs that didn't first come with his permission. Nothing has ever happened—good or evil, great or small—that he didn't know about and fully review first.

God is loving and generous, full of compassion and grace. He will be forever the faithful Father to his people, but he won't act as the senile grandfather. He won't be manipulated or used. What he does and allows will be according to his love for his creation. His severity will reveal how serious he is about driving us to our intended destination. He permits virtually anything to happen to us if it contributes to our good ending and happy destiny.

We may at some point misperceive him as heartless and cruel, but he won't be persuaded by our complaining, blaming, or resentment. He won't waver from his eternal purposes just so we'll think better of him along the way. Thankfully nor will he wash his hands of us because of our weak faith and myopic vision of what he is doing.

Consider this classic illustration from the Old Testament book of Ruth. There was a famine in the land of Judah during the time of the Judges. Elimelech, a Jew of Bethlehem, left Judah and moved his wife and two sons to dwell among the Moabites, a traditional enemy of Israel. Not a brilliant decision. After ten years, Elimelech and both of his sons died, leaving only his wife, Naomi, and her two Moabite daughters-in-law.

Destitute without a husband or sons, Naomi sets out to travel back home to Judah, as she has heard that God had provided food for his people there. Ruth, one of the two young women, follows Naomi, and the other daughter-in-law chooses to stay with her own people. Naomi repeatedly expresses deep bitterness and resentment toward God for turning his hand against her and dealing with her so cruelly.

When they arrive in Judah during barley harvest, Naomi advises Ruth to go into one of the fields to pick up any scraps left behind by the harvesters. But then an amazing "coincidence" occurs. The field she chooses just happens to be that of Boaz, a prosperous landowner and relative of Elimelech. Ruth eventually meets and marries Boaz, and the fortunes of Naomi and Ruth are dramatically reversed.

Ruth becomes very important for Jewish history. She gives birth to a son, Obed, who becomes the father of

Jesse, the father of David. So a Moabite—an alien and outsider of Israel—becomes part of the bloodline of Israel's greatest king and ultimately of Jesus of Nazareth. Think of the exquisite irony of this account, one full of complex interpenetrations of divine providence in the midst of human decisions and mistakes. Naomi, wholly unaware of the arrangement of events taking place around her, is overcome by her profound misreading of God's design for her. At the very moment she is complaining most and blaming God for his uncaring abandonment of her, at the height of her resentfulness and disillusionment, God is at work, setting the stage for the most lavish deliverance and blessing she could possibly have imagined.

And on a wider scale, through Naomi and Ruth, God was determining the future course of the Jewish people and the coming of the Messiah, all of which Naomi was totally unable to perceive. She became only partially aware of the lavish, over-the-top deliverance God had in mind for her. She was aware that God had provided her a "guardian-redeemer" who would look out for her in old age, something she had regarded as impossible (Ruth 4:14-17), but she wasn't aware that this would be an event that would continue the lineage of King David and Jesus (Matthew 1:1-16).

Ruth's great-grandson, King David, offered praises to God for such faithfulness and loving care:

You have searched me, Lord,
    and you know me.
You know when I sit and when I rise;
    you perceive my thoughts from afar.
You discern my going out and my lying down;
    you are familiar with all my ways.
Before a word is on my tongue
    you, Lord, know it completely.
You hem me in behind and before,
    you lay your hand upon me.
Such knowledge is too wonderful for me,
    too lofty for me to attain.

Where can I go from your Spirit?
    Where can I flee from your presence?
If I go up to the heavens, you are there;
    if I make my bed in the depths, you are there.
If I rise on the wings of the dawn,
    if I settle on the far side of the sea,
even there your hand will guide me,
    your right hand will hold me fast.
                    (Psalm 139:1-10)

Here's the takeaway: God has so arranged things that the very best thing we could ever find in this world is his perfect will. That's why we're *commanded* to obey him. He knows that we can't possibly achieve our highest dreams and deepest longings without following him, so he commands us to do the very thing that will lead to our fulfillment and joy. And it gets even better; he also grants us the power to go the distance.

We're very spoiled and don't even know it. Most of us, at least in Western nations, have been raised directly or indirectly on the ideas of the Bible. We imagine a God who is loving and purposeful, a God who looks kindly upon his creatures. Unlike the ancient Greeks and Romans, whose gods and goddesses loved to toy with— or even abuse—human beings just for the fun of it, we have a Father who is enormously loving and indescribably generous and merciful.

In our profoundly limited vision of things, we'll forever mistake the fulfillment of our dreams and longings for the mirages that lie before us. What appears to be the Promised Land just ahead is often merely an illusion in the desert. We run full-steam ahead in pursuit of what isn't there, imagining that earthly bliss and personal fulfillment lie before us. We disregard the commandments and warnings of God along the way, thinking them to be roadblocks to our happiness, completely unaware that in reality they're the guardrails along the road.

Only later, provided we don't stop and turn on him in anger and resentment, does it dawn on us that the things he has allowed to come our way he intended for our good. The fact that they appear to us at the moment as evils is irrelevant. He takes the heat and accepts all our misperceptions and accusations of his "cruelty" or "indifference" or "absence" or anything else that in our pain we choose to hurl at him.

This all-consuming purpose of God is to lead us to reconciliation and salvation, and this entails not just happy and pleasant circumstances. It usually involves some elements of temporal judgment and discipline aimed in our direction because we typically don't obey very willingly. Just like a responsible parent, often God will employ measures to get our attention or to keep us on track.

You may not recognize the name of John Newton, but you no doubt know of the famous hymn "Amazing Grace." One of the cruelest, most stubbornly rebellious and slow-learning men of the eighteenth century, Newton moved for many years from one ridiculous folly to another. He stumbled and fumbled through life, coming to the brink of disaster and death too many times to count, but he was rescued repeatedly (and dramatically) by the unseen hand of God.

Newton became very familiar with pain, sorrow, frustration, abuse by others, danger, and near-death experiences as he continued to pursue his self-willed recklessness. In reading about his life before conversion, you can't help noticing that every pain allowed to come his way was in reality the divine signature placed upon his life, for God's divine judgment is designed to lead us to repentance and life. What is too often thought to be God's hatred or wrath toward us is actually his love in keeping us from going over the cliff—permanently.

After many years of discipline, Newton finally understood that God would never give up on him. In the end, God had his way. When Newton looked back on his life, he saw that every trial and tribulation he went through was exactly what he needed to be brought into the kingdom of God. What followed was a long and fruitful life of service, and some of the greatest hymns of praise and gratitude ever written came from his pen. We still sing the words of his personal confession:

> Amazing grace, how sweet the sound,
> That saved a wretch like me.
> I once was lost, but now am found,
> Was blind but now I see.
>
> Through many dangers, toils and snares,
> I have already come.
> 'Tis grace hath brought me safe thus far,
> And grace will lead me home.[1]

What was true for John Newton was true for us: sin and rebellion have their consequences, but God intends for those consequences to lead to our ultimate good. The New Testament letter of Hebrews explains it this way: "[Our fathers] disciplined us for a little while as they thought best; but God disciplines us for our good, in order that we may share in his holiness" (Hebrews 12:10).

Incidentally, we can believe firmly in divine judgments in history without being able to point out just where those judgments are occurring. I can't say, for example, that your problems are cases of God's judgment, in the same way that you can't say the same about mine. Often, such things are hidden from us. If God chooses to tell us about them in more detail, then so be it, but we can plan on experiencing God's ongoing discipline for the ultimate purpose of our growth. Typically, this growth comes through resistance, but for the believer, every bad thing that happens, whether originating from sinful behavior or not, becomes raw material in the hands of the Creator in order to manufacture something good.

It is the occupation of a lifetime to learn this lesson: What God has in mind for us is our good—our total good, our highest good for all eternity. This truth usually comes to us after years of trial and error, years of ups and downs, years of coming in and out the doors of the church, of rising to heights of faith and joy, and sometimes plunging into the depths of despair and resentment.

If anyone has just cause for resentment, it would be God, for all that he endures from us! Yet he keeps totally focused and knows exactly what he's doing at all times. He doesn't allow our blindness or self-pity to distract him from what he knows to be the only road that will get us home.

Why Does God Permit So Much Evil?

God has all power and all knowledge and is second to none. No equals and no competitors. The fact that evil is rampant in his creation is no surprise to him. It's there only by permission. From time to time, evil may seem to be running wild, but in fact it's always on a leash. And we should be grateful that we've never seen how bad it could become.

Exactly why God allows evil in his creation, he doesn't bother to tell us, and he doesn't need to. He is God. We can't understand everything about God, but we have enough information to satisfy many of our basic questions. In many cases, God chooses to let us go through whatever evil or trouble we may be facing at the moment. He could have prevented it and allowed us an easy skate, rather than the tough slog some have to endure. He could end it entirely but probably won't until he's through using it for his purposes.

If we take a close look at both the Old and New testaments, we notice something interesting about evil's presence in the world. It is considered an intruder into God's good creation but is allowed to prowl about for a time, and with a considerable degree of freedom. Yet it's always within bounds.

Sometimes it may look as though it exceeds all limits, and whereas good often seems to run out of steam, evil seems never to tire. But just when we think God's hands are tied, he yanks the chain and brings it to heel. He is ruler of all. Evil is evil and good is good, but whereas God never uses good for evil purposes, he often uses or blatantly exploits evil for good purposes. He does this by turning it upside down and inside out.

The stories of the patriarchs in Genesis are wonderful illustrations of evil being exploited for good. One of the clearest pictures comes to us in the account of Joseph. Young Joseph is mistreated, violently abused, tricked, kidnapped, enslaved, falsely accused, and imprisoned. Yet every time he is kicked and abused, he is mysteriously bumped up one more rung of the ladder. He moves from the deep hole in the beginning of the story to the position of the prime minister of Egypt at the end.

God used all the evil directed toward Joseph as raw material to construct not only his preservation from starvation and death but also the rescue of those who abused him as well as the salvation of the entire nation he served. As Joseph says, "You intended to harm me, but God intended it for good to accomplish what is now being done, the saving of many lives" (Genesis 50:20).

This pattern presented early in the Bible became the blueprint for how God has chosen to deal with evil in his realm for the rest of history. He may permit a certain amount of wickedness to occur, but he always reserves the right to twist and use it for his own purposes. We see the same design in the New Testament.

Through Jesus, we observe the ultimate example of this long-established pattern. Jesus is falsely accused, abused, arrested, slandered, tortured, and then murdered. In the end, this greatest of all evils served to provide the way of salvation, not only for all his followers, but also for some of his enemies who eventually came to repentance, forgiveness, and faith in him. It was, in many respects, a reenactment of the Joseph story.

What we see in Genesis continues throughout early church history, through the centuries of the martyrs, in the subsequent eras of the church, and up to the present day. This is God's will for the remainder of time until he brings down the curtain and calls humanity to final judgment. After every tiny scrap of evil is dealt with in the complete justice and fairness of God, he intends to re-create a new heaven and new earth where evil is no longer even a possibility—where only goodness and righteousness will exist.

The manipulation of evil for good ends is one of the most exciting aspects of God's program on earth. He uses the bad things around us in ways we couldn't possibly expect. He brings good out of the bad not *in spite of* it but *because of* it.

Let's consider a few very earthly and human analogies of this. For example, it's common practice to exploit the intentions of others for our own ends in a variety of ways. Consider the game of chess. As the competition progresses, the better of the two players cleverly ascertains his opponent's game plan. He has two options. He can block and frustrate the plan immediately, or he can so arrange his own strategy to account for it, to absorb it. In this way, while his opponent is cheerfully fulfilling his own scheme, he's also unwittingly fulfilling that of the superior player. Just when he thinks he's about to proclaim victory, he's suddenly checkmated. The game is over.

Here's another example. By means of electronic surveillance, the intelligence wing of Government A discovers a secret source of critical inside information on Government B. To its dismay, Government B discovers that its code has been broken. Rather than change the code, the leaders decide to feed bogus information to Government A so that their enemies will devise a military strategy based upon this false information. This enables the leaders of Government B to make counterplans to frustrate the enemy and win the conflict. Both are realizing their intentions, but one is exploiting the strategy of the other for its own ends and victory. The same thing occurs in football games or boardroom maneuvers of the business world. One side moves forward with its carefully orchestrated scheme only to find later that it has perfectly and unwittingly played into the higher, better planned strategy of the other side.

So it is with God. He's the Grand Master of chess, who can at any moment impose his own plan over ours (or anyone else's), so that no matter what, he can bring the game to his own decreed conclusion. We may deliberately live a life of rebellion and selfishness, discarding his will at every point, or we may live a life of Spirit-empowered obedience and self-sacrifice. Whichever course we take, he wins in the end. By scripting his own plot to overarch ours, he allows us to fulfill our plans but ultimately to bring about his will. In this way, evil is both exploited as well as judged, good is rewarded, and God is the victor.

Of course, I've not used perfect analogies, since there are no exact earthly parallels to how God's nature and sovereignty are involved in human life. God is entirely unique and profoundly mysterious. He is revealed to us only in part. As I said, this revelation isn't everything we want to know, but it's enough to grasp the basics of what he wants us to know. The main point of comparison here is that the superior being uses the activities of the inferior for his own will.

To drive home the point, let's explore a few concrete illustrations from modern history. First, consider Argentina. Prior to 1982, the nation was very slow to accept the gospel message. Christian preachers and missionaries were ignored, and very little spiritual fruit was evident. After that year, however, everything changed dramatically. Widespread spiritual awakenings took place in a rather short period of time. What made the difference? The Falkland War.

In the conflict involving Argentina's Falkland Islands, Great Britain gained a quick and decisive victory. The national pride that had kept Argentina from coming humbly to God in repentance was brought very low in just a few days. The nation was stunned and humiliated. Spiritual leaders in the land observed that this shattered pride began to open the door to the message of repentance and reconciliation in a way that nothing had before. According to Peter Wagner, missionary and former Professor of Church Growth at the Fuller Theological Seminary's School of World Missions, all this came about not *in spite of* the war but *because of* it.[2]

Something similar happened in Afghanistan. In the years prior to the breakup of the Soviet Union, Soviet authorities made a practice of punishing soldiers in its ranks who identified as Christians. According to some reports, one form of punishment was to be sent to the front in Afghanistan, where the Soviets were fighting a very frustrating and seemingly endless battle. They figured this was a good way of killing two birds with one stone. They could weed out Christians and still continue to occupy Afghanistan.

When the Russian troops finally gave up the battle and pulled out of Afghanistan in 1989, they left behind small groups of Muslims who were interested in learning more about Jesus. In this way, much mission work was accomplished. Without realizing it, and entirely against their intent, an atheistic government effectively functioned as a mission board to the Afghans. They played out their chess game, but heaven's Chess Master simply turned their strategy to his own advantage.[3]

Over the years, our family has discovered that some of the best things that ever happened to us came as a direct result of the worst things that ever happened to us. If we take the apostle Paul seriously "that in all things God works for the good of those who love him, who have been called according to his purpose" (Romans 8:28), then we'll eventually see how God still writes his superior, more sophisticated script over all others.

No matter what evils befall us, good (even excellence) may be brought out of them. This is one of God's favorite things to do. This point is too important to pass over lightly.

If you forget most of what this book says, don't forget this; just as it is Satan's purpose to take all that is good and turn it toward evil ends, so it is God's purpose to take all that is evil in the lives of those who love him and turn it for good. The commandeering and exploitation of evil for good is one of the most powerful aspects of God's strategies on earth. He skillfully manipulates the bad things around us in ways we couldn't possibly expect or imagine.

We need to fix this truth in our minds. Between now and the final act of history's play, as mentioned before, God has determined to allow evil to roam about on a chain, not free to do anything and everything it wants, but to do much that we wouldn't want. Evil will always be an intruder and an invader. As long as we dwell on this planet, we'll always live in occupied territory. Evil will be relatively free (within God's prescribed limits), but it will always be under the ongoing judgment of the Ruler of all things. Each and every day he will choose to exploit what evil determines to do and to turn it toward his good purposes. Again, evil will continue to accuse, blame, abuse, misrepresent the truth, destroy, and pillage, but it will remain on a leash. It will never be totally free and will do no more than it's allowed to do. God defeats it handily, takes it prisoner, and redirects it to bring the good he intends.

Why do I repeat myself? Simply to underscore this critical point: whether people choose to do evil or good in this life, God has decreed that he will write his will into the script of human history and bring it to its conclusion in exactly the way he has purposed.

Ultimately, all evil will be rooted out of God's creation and destroyed forever, never to again raise its head. It's now under an absolute death sentence and will not for any reason fail to keep its date with execution.

We can oppose God's will and do the most terrible things, or we can do everything in our power to try to please him. In either case, he's able to enter into our own worldly troubles and sins and in some mysterious way bring out of them ultimate good—both his and ours. Without doubt, evil, and all those who love it and are given to it, will face judgment and destruction. But it is to God's glory that we turn from it and live.

Gaining a Wider Perspective

Whatever happens to us, whether storm, disaster, heartbreak, death, flood, plague, war, or famine, God will bring about the good he intends for us. We may be blind to it, we may be late in recognizing it, or we may choose not to see it at all. But his purpose is to enter into the catastrophes of our lives and draw out of them what he has determined long before the foundation of the world (Ephesians 1:1-14).

So whether we suffer or not, whether we are successful and happy on this earth or not, whether we stumble, fail, or sin, we can still be drawn into God's ultimate purposes for good. It's all his doing and not ours. We can be sure of his long-term faithfulness and his stubborn insistence that we arrive safely on the shores of his eternal kingdom. We can trust that we as believers will dwell happily in his presence forever.

Does all this sound like wishful thinking or self-delusion? If so, I encourage you to give these ideas some time to sink in, because in my experience, it becomes far more believable after years of personal experience than at the beginning of our faith journey. Why? Because we see things better from a distance. In order to see the big picture, we need to get a long perspective on the plan of God. When we look back one day on this tragedy or that, we can say, "Thank you, Lord, for stopping that wedding." "Thank you for keeping me from being accepted by that school." Even "Thank you for that year-long illness I had as a child."

It's absolutely essential that we stick around long enough to see the drama play out. We can't walk out after the first two acts because they weren't to our liking and then complain that it didn't come out right. The only way to evaluate a story is from its end. Cherish this truth: God loves to bring the very good out of the very bad. He seems to delight in creating and manipulating circumstances to preserve and rescue us at the last minute just when we think everything is lost. He wants us to see that he's there and that he truly does have something wonderful in mind for us. He's the only Being in the universe who is able to create something out of nothing (in theological terms, *ex nihilo*). He's ready to swing open a wide exit from Calamityville or pave a new road out of Misery City, just at that moment when we're convinced that there's absolutely no exit.

This is one of the reasons he allows troubles to come our way. He expects us to cry out to him for help and then to look for the way he is opening up for us (Psalm 50:15). Such experiences pump up our faith and move us further down the road to spiritual adulthood.

If you've never read anything from Charles Spurgeon's devotional book *Morning and Evening*, I would like you to read this excerpt based on "the trial of your faith" (1 Peter 1:7):

> Faith untried may be true faith, but it is sure to be
> little faith, and it is likely to remain dwarfish so long
> as it is without trials. Faith never prospers so well as
> when all things are against her: tempests are her train-
> ers, and lightnings are her illuminators....
>
> Tried faith brings experience. You could not
> have believed your own weakness had you not been
> compelled to pass through the rivers; and you would
> never have known God's strength had you not been

supported amid the water-floods. Faith increases in solidity, assurance, and intensity, the more it is exercised with tribulation. Faith is precious, and its trial is precious too.

Let not this, however, discourage those who are young in faith. You will have trials enough without seeking them: the full portion will be measured out to you in due season. Meanwhile, if you cannot yet claim the result of long experience, thank God for what grace you have; praise him for that degree of holy confidence whereunto you have attained: walk according to that rule, and you shall yet have more and more of the blessing of God, till your faith shall remove mountains and conquer impossibilities.[4]

Recognizing God at Work

We can have our faith increased (or restored) and our resentment decreased as we gain more knowledge and experience of God's ways. With each passing year, filled with both happy events and puzzling ordeals (even pain and sorrow), our perspective of what God is like and what he's doing should grow. There are a number of ways this can happen.

One way we come to a greater understanding of him is to read. We can read the Bible, biographies of Christians, stories behind the hymns we sing, accounts of missionaries—anything that tells us more about the God of the Bible. We can even read good fiction or history books that show us who our God is.

One of the values of reading the Bible is to see his great works in the lives of those who have gone before us. We have the privilege of tracking the experiences of those who lived thousands of years ago, people who claimed that there was a God who got involved in their lives in the most remarkable ways. Ask yourself this question: Why would so many people from so many different backgrounds and generations report that some invisible but powerful person was clearly present, helping them out of their troubles or saving their lives?

These people weren't in the habit of sitting down comfortably in the midst of war, turmoil, death, disease, and starvation just to say nice things about life. They weren't so bored that they wanted to create poetry or prose to speak of a God they wished for, but who wasn't really there. The very fact that we possess a thick book of testimonies claiming God was there, that he took an active part in their lives, that he rescued them repeatedly, that he answered prayers and communicated with them over a long period of time, means something. Such books don't just pop into existence by pure chance or sheer randomness.

What would these many writers stand to gain by making claims that weren't true? For their witness, they were routinely mistreated, ostracized, bullied, enslaved, tortured, and even brutally killed. The histories of the Jewish people and Christians are full of horrific forms of genocide and persecution on a wide scale, over long stretches of time. Persecution of believers continues to this day in many parts of the world.

Even if people choose to deny that there's anything supernatural about the Bible and its composition, they're still confronted with the fact that a great many people over the centuries have continued to affirm the unchanging truths about God's help—even in the face of fiercest opposition.

The same could be said for the enormous number of history books written about believers. Apart from the Bible are thousands of believers' autobiographies and biographies. Each of these books testify to God's daily faithfulness and provision. How can the existence of such a vast treasure of literature be explained, except that there must be something to the unusual claims? At the very least, it's worth checking into.

In addition to the Bible and the biographies of believers, we can look to the inspiring songs we sing each worship service. The abundance of hymns composed over the centuries reads like the life journals of the composers. All of them tell the same thing: There is a God who is faithful; he looks after us; he comforts us in our sorrows; he invades our lives with love and joy; he heals, protects, and rescues us; he communicates to us in clear, unmistakable ways. The Christian hymnbook is a powerful source of corroborative evidence in support of the Bible's assertions about God's care for us.

There's more. We can learn about God's character and attributes by studying stars, animals, trees, rocks, insects, molecules, or absolutely anything else he made. The more we come to know about the things around us, the more we can appreciate the high degree of complexity and design within them. If we're honest and pay attention long enough to what is around us and within us, we'll eventually come to conclude that there's more to the universe than what we might at first perceive. Design and purpose emerge as we study what is right in front of us.

Seeing God's Hand at Work in Our Lives

As we continue down the road to more knowledge, we arrive at new conclusions about the God who made all this. The more we contemplate our world and our lives, the more we come to see how deeply God is involved in our own histories. If you're a borderline believer, or someone who can no longer see any clear signs of God's presence, keep replaying the tape of your life. Dig deep. Start remembering and listing the evidences of someone else behind the scenes.

Begin with your very first memory of getting through

a tough situation. What do you see when you were in any danger? Did someone suddenly come to your rescue? When you needed a friend, did someone befriend you? Did some fortunate or surprising turn of events come your way at just the right moment? Think hard about this. Most of the ways God walks with us and cares for us are not miraculous but seemingly rather mundane. Our experiences of discovering (or rediscovering) God are tailor-made for us by him.

One friend of mine came to faith and entered the preaching ministry in a remarkable way. While studying at a local college to become a disc jockey, he earned extra money as the lead sound technician of the school's auditorium. One day he was asked to supervise the sound system at a Jesus Rally to be held at the college. He didn't know what a Jesus Rally was; he only knew that he wanted nothing to do with it! So he tried his best to find someone else to engineer the sound. None of his usual assistants was available, and he found himself stuck with the job.

During the team meeting prior to the event, there was an extended time of prayer. For a full hour (he didn't even know that anyone *ever* prayed for an entire hour), many people around him kept saying out loud, "Thank you, Lord," or, "Thank you, Jesus, for all that you've done." Not wanting to stand out in the crowd, he decided to say something similar. "Thank you, Jesus!" he said loudly, just in fun.

But the minute he said this, something strange happened. It struck him like a bolt of lightning: he had many things to be thankful for. A number of great gifts had come his way over the years, but he had no idea whom to thank. It was as if the Almighty himself was addressing him in those moments. For the first time in his life, the blinders were removed, and he knew beyond a shadow of a doubt that God was the Source of all the good that had come to him. God's hand was behind everything he had ever received.

This revelation of God's care overwhelmed him. He left the auditorium that night as quickly as possible. When he reached his room, he dropped to his knees and said, "God, if you're there, if you're listening, I thank you for all that you've done for me. If you have a purpose for me, I'm yours." The next day he went to the college registrar and changed his major to religious studies. After graduation, he enrolled in seminary, was eventually ordained, and now is a pastor.

The New Testament teaches that God is happy to give good gifts to people, even to those who care nothing about him, or even to evil people who are hostile to the very idea of God. He sends his rain upon the just and the unjust (Matthew 5:45) and is kind to the ungrateful and the wicked (Luke 6:35). God wants us (even paves the way for us) to be curious enough about the Source and Sender of these good things to search after him (Acts 17:24-28).

As we continually pursue more truth about God and his purpose for our lives, we'll come to see and appreciate things we couldn't perceive before. And as we reach each new level of spiritual insight and maturity, we can play our life's tape again and understand even more. This process of reevaluation, done dozens or even hundreds of times throughout our lives, enables us to detect more of the divine clues around us.

In counseling people of all levels of experience, who tell me they are still having trouble seeing God's involvement, I ask them to give me a history of their lives. I ask them to remember even the tiny details of the events that shaped them most. As they speak, I point out things that appear to me to be divine footprints. "Oh, I've never considered that before," is the usual response. "That *could* have been God!" The new thought sets their minds in motion. When they return for the next appointment, they bring with them a list of more things they discovered about God's active presence in their lives.

It has been said that God brings us the provisions we need even while we sleep. Happily, he protects us and cares for us in ways we don't even know at the time we're going through a dark phase of life. Only a careful backward glance will reveal to us the ways he imparts his many gifts.

Faith thrives on reality, the reality of events in real time and space, and the events that happen to us in the turbulence of daily life.

I love seeing this in the life of missionary Hudson Taylor. One day, while waiting to journey up one of the inland rivers of China, he encountered a rainstorm. It was so severe that he found it necessary to stay on his small craft for the night, which was tied securely to the dock. Being so tired from his constant labors, and with an injured knee, he considered the storm to be a gift, a mini-vacation from God. As soon as the rain let up, a crew member went into town to pick up some laundry and discovered that hired men had been searching for them all night. Misinformed, they thought Hudson's boat held opium and were going to demand that he either split the profits with them or be killed. Thankfully, the torrential rain of the day before had kept him in the boat and the men from seeing two feet in front of them. Hudson's life was spared.[5]

Deliverances and rescues of all kinds occur with such regularity in the lives of God's people that explaining them merely as "coincidences" becomes increasingly far-fetched and silly. We'll probably never realize in this life all the times God was bringing us provisions for living while we were sleeping, or daydreaming, or just going about our daily business—maybe even while we were complaining about and blaming him or doing something entirely against his will.

Not only is there a long history of people who admitted to receiving help from God in times of need or danger, but there's also an equally long history of those who trusted in false gods and found them wanting. For every person declaring the God of the Bible to be reliable and faithful, there's someone else declaring the false gods and idols of the world to be totally worthless and unreliable. In this way, God receives a double testimony.

Our Tragedies Are the Subplot

History books remind us that we can't create our own gods out of thin air and expect them to do something positive for us. People may like to manufacture their own deities that suit their preferences and lifestyles, but when we desperately need concrete help in times of real trouble, these gods can be counted on to go AWOL. When you're in a lifeboat surrounded by hungry sharks, you need a lot more than a homemade deity.

Rather than throw God away if things aren't going the way you think they should, keep in mind that the timetable of God's rescues and reversals is firmly within his own will, purpose, and timetable. He alone chooses whom, when, and in what way rescues take place. What we can learn from a lifetime experience of God is that whether he rescues, delays, or decides to bring us home, his ways are always just and good.

I think we can all agree that the best part about a problem is when it's over! How happy we are to emerge from a long, dark tunnel with more or less everything intact, much like the first day after a high fever passes. But the real benefit is in looking back upon it *after* our perspective changes. Scripture constantly attests that when we live according to God's purpose, he will be with us in all our life's storms and pilots our little boats into safe harbors. He brings things to pass at a time and in such a way that each and every sorrow and struggle is eventually used for our benefit. Every grief he can turn into a blessing. Hearing all this on life's bright and sunny days sounds good, but there are times when it doesn't seem to help in the slightest. Some days this kind of thinking only irritates us.

When suffering goes so deep that life doesn't even seem worth living another day, hearing that our grief will be exploited for our good sometime in the distant future carries little weight with us. The problem is that only time will teach us this lesson about suffering. That's why the life of faith is described in faith literature (including the Bible) as a "way" or a long journey. Until the day comes when we're able to reach either some near or distant happy destination, we're often unable to see any of the benefits of the high, craggy mountains and the dry, desolate valleys.

But don't bail out too soon! The Christian life is a full marathon, not a hundred-yard dash. This is the piece of wisdom my family and I have learned over years in ministry. There have been plenty of days when we were more than willing to leave the place where we were laboring. Often we wanted not to spend another minute doing what we were doing where we were doing it, but Someone kept encouraging us, "Stay around and see what happens." It was only in the staying around that we were able to see what God was doing behind the scenes all along. I'll have to admit that there were a few times we didn't wait; we bolted and ended up in a far worse situation.

If ever there were a biblical character who could easily have wallowed in regret and resentment, it was Esau, the brother of Jacob (see Genesis 25–33). Esau was a rugged outdoorsman who, in an hour of weakness, traded his birthright to his slimy, manipulating, wimpy brother. All he got out of it was a bowl of lentils. He was so hungry from his time in the fields that he was willing to give up anything for momentary relief.

At first glance, Esau appears to be a person of such major stupidity that there couldn't be any useful lesson for us. But at a closer look, he turns out to be not the rare exception but the rule—the typical modern person. Far from being too much of a dimwit to be an example for us today, he's closer to qualifying as the patron saint of our world. Like so many of us today, in utter folly he gives up all that is of any real, lasting value for a bowl of soup—a momentary pleasure, an empty glory, relief.

As a matter of routine, people throw away lifelong marriages and their families for just one night of supposed pleasure. They end promising careers with an offhanded, angry, or ill-thought word. More profoundly, they trade the possibility of eternal joy for a life of selfish ease and self-glorification.

Not only was Esau foolish, he was also a victim. He was tricked not once but twice. His brother Jacob cheated him out of his birthright (the ancient version of one's inheritance, insurance policy, and retirement plan all wrapped into one), but with his mother's help, Jacob also manipulated circumstances to deceive and receive his father's life blessing, something intended solely for the firstborn son. This blessing from the father was of incalculable worth to the young men of his day. Without it, life would not be the same. Esau could manage somehow to prosper without his birthright, but in the culture of his day, he couldn't get very far without the blessing of the firstborn.

As the story goes, Jacob and Esau parted ways (Jacob fled in order to survive) and didn't see each other again for many years. Jacob became very successful and wealthy, while Esau disappeared from the scene entirely. But then something happens that the reader doesn't expect. One day someone comes to Jacob and informs him that his brother is on his way. This wasn't good news, but it gets even worse. He is told that Esau was coming with four hundred men.

Jacob, still the unmanly, slimy wimp that he always was, sends his servants and herds ahead to meet him, heavily laden with gifts, in order to soften up and absorb his brother's wrath. But what happens when Esau finally appears stuns everyone. He comes not with wrath and vengeance in mind, but with reconciliation and friendship. We don't know exactly what happened to Esau in those hidden years, but we can deduce that God had so lavishly blessed him that he held no grudges against his brother and needed none of the material gifts offered him.

Esau illustrates what can happen to people who make such a major life mistake that they can't recover from it. This also applies to victims of abuse, trickery, deception, and the gross selfishness of others. If we can put our abuse in the hands of our Maker, miraculous things can happen. When we are backed into a corner with absolutely no way out and nowhere to go, when there's not a single human solution to our problem, one of God's favorite activities to create an out for us.

This is also the pattern illustrated in the Hebrew exodus from Egypt. God not only manufactured an exit but also provided a Promised Land on the other end. Without a Promised Land, we have only an *exit*, a momentary escape from the problem. In his providence, what he wills is far more than an exit. He wants for us an *exodus*—an *out* that also comes with an *in*—a full deliverance that's part of both an earthly as well as an eternal purpose.

Let's face it. We're blamers, and it's not uncommon for us to walk out on God in disgust and resentment for something that's happened. And now, perhaps years later, we've come to recognize that something good was actually in store for us all along, but we are now too ashamed of our behavior to come back to God in thankfulness. If that is you, remember God has big shoulders. He doesn't slink off and sulk in the corner feeling sorry for himself. Rather, he's the forgiving, waiting Father wonderfully portrayed in Jesus's famous parable of the prodigal son who comes home (see Luke 15:11-32).

Nothing that happens shocks God. He isn't stunned or thrown off balance by our petulance, bad reactions, and misunderstandings of him. He has been through it all before. What we do or think has been done or thought millions of times by others before us. The amazing thing about God is that he doesn't hold a grudge against us. We may walk out on him one day, but he's delighted when we walk back in the next. Sometimes, it takes years for us to work through our misperceptions of him and to return. We shouldn't feel too ashamed or proud to come back. A simple, but totally sincere, "I'm so sorry, Lord. Please forgive me!" can, in an instant, neutralize all alienation from him.

Years of our lives can be utterly wasted on deep bitterness and rage against God before we realize that he had something good in mind from the beginning. Resentment for not being able to find a proper mate, living with some infirmity or deformity, failure to achieve a desired goal or honor, loss of a loved one, and thousands of other things can keep us from understanding God and his ways.

At the heart of the faith life is divine purpose, the beginning of real life. There we discover that our own temporary wishes and goals were not the main plot after all. They were merely subplots of something much greater. It is this understanding of God's best for our lives that has the power to overrule, overpower, and displace any stubborn resentment or bitterness in our lives that may have occupied our attention or won our highest allegiance.

Chapter 6

THE IMPORTANCE OF GOOD TEACHING

If you've ever been part of a large family (or a part of any organization, really), you'll understand how easily we can misunderstand one another and how those misunderstandings can blossom into hurt and resentment. A game of "he-said / she-said" begins and takes on a life of its own.

For example, adult siblings Joe and Megan both have ideas of where the family should go on vacation. Mom likes both suggestions, but Joe implies to Megan that Mom said she likes his idea much better. Megan is offended that Mom took Joe's side and starts to nurse that hurt into resentment. When Mom hears what Joe has done, she is not happy. But when she is able to convince the wounded Megan that she had never said anything of the sort, or had the opinion Joe relayed, Megan's resentment against her is dispelled.

But occasionally there is a situation when a mother just can't persuade one of her children of the truth. It is highly frustrating, even infuriating, that the embittered person seems either unable or unwilling to be dissuaded from a false view. They seem to have fallen in love with their resentment. Isn't it the same with us sometimes? We tend to nourish and eventually come to cherish our resentments. They become part of us somehow, and we don't want someone messing them up with the truth. Being human, sometimes when we think we've found the cause of all our troubles, and since we've already invested so much time and energy into our bitterness, we are very reluctant to relinquish it. Too often, this comes at the expense of our relationship with God.

The Illogic of Resentment

Once we find a good scapegoat for our problems and frustrations and hurt, we hate to say good-bye to it. We feel justified in our anger and hold on tight. At this point, our resentments and bitterness seem to take on a logic of their own. They appear to be so absolutely beyond contradiction, so totally accurate in their assessment of things, that nothing seems more reasonable than the way we view the situation, the motives, and the issues involved. We've seen how easy it is to blame someone close to us over some very basic misunderstanding. But when it comes to blaming God, we need to be even more cautious and wise.

We have an ever-present enemy who loves to suggest some evil intent on the part of our God. Satan doesn't go easy on people just because they doubt his existence. He is unrelenting in his commitment to deface, corrupt, and eventually destroy everything God has made. One of the names for Satan is "the Slanderer." It is one of his highest priorities to misrepresent God and to put an ugly twist on every word and action that comes from our Creator. His success is guaranteed every time he leaves us with some lasting doubts about God's goodness, wisdom, or purpose.

Here is a sobering example: more than 1,200 desperate people have jumped from San Francisco's Golden Gate Bridge since it first opened in 1937. On average, there has been one about every two weeks. In detailed studies done on those who somehow managed to survive the four-second, 220-foot drop to the Bay, the survivors tell strikingly similar stories. The common account is that immediately after the leap off the side of the bridge, something very strange and unexpected happens. Those who just a moment earlier couldn't think of a single reason to live, or who couldn't imagine any possible way out of their plight, suddenly, as if by some magic, realize a whole series of good and happy resolutions to their problems. But in their earlier, muddled misperceptions of reality and resentments of all kinds, all these answers had entirely escaped them. In the first few seconds of their free fall, they can see no way out. But then time seems to slow down and a high-speed tape begins to play in their minds. By the time they reach the last thirty feet above the cold water, they can clearly see a solution to every problem they face, except for one—the fact that they just jumped off the Golden Gate Bridge. Those who lived to tell about it reported that their last thought before hitting the water was, "I wish I hadn't done it!"[1] Tragically, for the vast majority who made the leap, this final revelation would have come too late.

It is all too easy to forget that life isn't given to us randomly, or as a smorgasbord of delights to be consumed and then forgotten. We're not here to be comfortable, to reach "self-realization," or to enlarge and enrich ourselves. We're here for reasons far exceeding our own. We were created for the express purpose of pleasing and glorifying God. Our time on earth is not primarily for our pleasure and enjoyment, even though much of it, thankfully, is enjoyable. But whether it is or not, we're still here for the same reason. We walk about in short or tall bodies, with beautiful or plain faces, in wealth or in want, in whatever skin color we were given at birth, and all of it is intended to play a role in the fulfillment of God's glory. If we miss this one point, we'll misperceive everything else that follows.

If there is such a thing as purgatory, it's not in the distant future after this earthly life, but in the here and now. According to the teaching of the New Testament, we're here for purging, for purification, for the long-term upward call toward the eternal City of God. As we progressively shed the sins that cling to us, we move toward life lived in the image of Jesus Christ. If we're repeatedly told that we exist for our own pleasure and comfort, for our own successes and interests, then we'll end up very disappointed and severely disillusioned. But if we understand early in our life journey that we exist for God's glory and purposes, then we'll be able to put into the right perspective the varied and unexpected things that happen to us on earth.

There's a critical point here about hard times that we need to understand. It's just not true, as some Christians believe, that Satan sends us the bad things and God sends us the good. Suffering doesn't come our way in opposition to God's will, but often because of it. The apostle Paul tells us that as God grants us faith, so he also grants us suffering (Philippians 1:29). As we talked about in the previous chapter, from the Bible's point of view, our suffering (and everything else that happens) first passes through the mind of God and is carefully reviewed for his approval.

No great saint ever became one by a walk in the park on a sunny afternoon. In biblical history, suffering has functioned as perhaps the most effective way of developing strong disciples. We love comfort and ease (we want lots of it!), but it doesn't do the job. Suffering either hardens us into blamers or softens us and matures us. It all depends upon how we understand and experience it.

Resentment against God and the paralyzing disillusionment that follows result when we don't grasp the fact that God is in charge of our lives. It is he who brings his will to bear in the bad as well as in the good. The good news is that however bad it may be on this side, God goes through it hand-in-hand with us, and it can't even be compared to the joy and glory of what awaits us on the other side.

Discovering Our Part to Play in God's Perfect Plan

The worst mistake we can make in life is to say, "I will decide what I'll do, where I'll go, and why. I expect God to be the wind in my sails that drives me to my goal, but I'll be the captain of my ship." God never intended for any of us to attempt the journey on our own steam, according to our micro-wisdom, following our own paths. He knows that powerful opposing forces around us are too great for anything we have in us to match them. I can't reiterate it enough—the driving theme for our lives on earth is that we don't exist for ourselves, but for a higher will and greater purpose than our own.

One of the life-transforming lessons the Bible teaches us is that our own personal will and goals can become important subplots in God's script, but they are definitely not the main plot. We live a very short segment of a story—a brief scene in an extended play—which has been going on since long before we arrived on this planet and which will continue long after we depart. What happens between the two points of birth and death can't be totally understood and reconciled in this life.

Our lives are much like a mystery or spy novel. What appears to make sense in the early chapters often turns out to be a complete misperception. What we think we understand for the moment may be far off the mark when seen in the light of the startling conclusion. This is often bad news to those among us who see themselves as the center of the universe or imagine that they call the shots as rulers of their own kingdoms. Whether we admit it or not, we often live as though everything in the world orbits around us—that it all exists for our good or pleasure. So when this "me-first" lifestyle hits the rocks, we become unbearable to live with.

The I'll-do-it-my-way approach to life is one of the results of humankind's original Fall (Genesis 3). Since then, we've tried to construct our own realities, make our own rules, and pretend that there is no God who has a very specific plan for us and who wants us to know what it is. But how exciting and liberating is the realization that we don't exist for ourselves! To discover that we are here on this earth by design, not by chance, and we leave only by divine arrangement, not by "accident" or "natural causes." The boundaries of when and where we live are decreed by God long before we ever arrive (Acts 17:26), and the things that happen to us are never a surprise to the One who called us into being. This means that even when we run out of reasons to live, there is one extremely good reason to keep going. In the Westminster Shorter Catechism, we are reminded of what that reason is: "Man's chief end is to glorify God and enjoy him forever."[2]

One of the mottos of the Reformation is the Latin phrase *Soli Deo Gloria*—"glory to God alone." These few words summarize the Bible's view of our existence: We were created to live in a way that magnifies and pleases our Creator. He expects and helps us to find various, creative ways to exalt, honor, and satisfy him. He and his will (and the enjoyment of them both) are to be the central focus of human life.

Over the years, I've heard the accusation that such a God who creates us merely to please and exalt himself must be completely selfish. So why would we worship such a God? This criticism would be true only if God were like us. If God were essentially a selfish being, whose will was forever turned toward self-admiration at the expense and devaluation of others, this judgment would be entirely correct. But the happy news is the exact opposite; God has so constructed the universe that his glory and pleasure are also of the greatest benefit for every creature in it. His pleasure is by definition our highest good. What we can imagine as most advantageous and profitable for ourselves becomes a faint image compared to what God has in mind for us.

When God spoke to the prophet Jeremiah, he spelled out his plan for his people following a time of painful (but well-deserved) judgment: "'For I know the plans I have for you,' declares the LORD, 'plans to prosper you and not to harm you, plans to give you hope and a future. Then you will call on me and come and pray to me, and I will listen to you. You will seek me and find me when you seek me with all your heart'" (Jeremiah 29:11-13). These words were originally for Jeremiah and about the people of Israel, but in the subsequent centuries of faith experience, Christians have found them to be true for them as well.

In our chronic misperceptions of God, we foolishly imagine that a life pleasing to God would be completely devoid of fun, vitality, good taste, culture, adventure, physical pleasure, humor, celebration, and everything else that we love and seek. No doubt the behavior of religious people around the world, including much of what we know as "church life," contributes to this dismal portrayal of the faith life. The reputation of Christianity depends in part upon its attractiveness to those living in a dark world. That attractiveness lies not in the beauty of its church buildings, the scope of its programs, or the glitz of its advertising, but rather in the electrifying behavior of its real believers. Nothing can take its place. The church person who sends the message that faith means sour-faced judgment upon all that is fun and exhilarating helps create the tragically false impression that what God has in mind for us is not life but "religion." That is dark-draped, sad-faced, funeral-home Christianity. This is the precise opposite of the truth.

Consider a few of the images that Jesus provides for us when he talks about the Father in heaven. In John 2:1-11, Jesus attends the wedding in the town of Cana. The hosts run out of wine (which was one of the worst things that could happen at an important gathering in ancient Palestine) and Jesus hears of the problem. Jesus could have done either of two things. He could have said, as many pious Christians would, "Well, you shouldn't be drinking such things in the first place. You carnal, pleasure-seeking wretches deserve to run out of wine." Or he could have taken the view that running out of wine during a huge wedding party with important guests is a very embarrassing thing, which he did. There were sophisticated wine connoisseurs present then, just as there might be now in some of our great dinner parties. Jesus took charge and chose the vintage. He created the one that would pass the inspection of the toughest and most discriminating wine taster. He transformed some large jars of rather bad water into the finest wine. "You saved the best for last!" the man who knew wine exclaimed to his host. Incidentally, this idea of saving the very best for last lies at the heart of the gospel's vision of human destiny. It's also worth noting here that the first of Jesus's signs, or miracles, was not for the purpose of any life and death emergency but only to save a friend from a social embarrassment. This shows that he cares about every single detail of our lives.

Jesus and his disciples were accused by others of being wine guzzlers (Matthew 11:19). When he and his disciples feasted rather than fasted, he explained that there is plenty of time for fasting when the party's over, but as long as the life of the party is present, then feasting is the order of the day (Matthew 9:14-15). Jesus brought the party with him wherever he went. This is one reason why the image of the great dinner gala—or the lavish, abundant feast—became one the leading pictures in the Gospels of the presence of God's kingdom. Jesus also tells the parable of a rebellious son who returns home from a life of dissipation and foolishness. The father orders not a time of fasting with grim and arduous penance for him but rather a great banquet in honor of his return (Luke 15:11-32).

Such illustrations are intended to tell us something about God. What does he have in mind for us? Not miserable, boring, rule-keeping religion, but joyful celebration that glorifies him and allows us to enjoy him. God is glorified when he is enjoyed and enjoyed when he is glorified. The two always go together. It's the expressed will of God for his creatures to find their highest pleasures and hearts' desires fulfilled in his highest purposes for them. All this is true because we are so important to God.

But in the Middle Ages there was a powerful ascetic movement in the church known as monasticism. Highly dedicated monks would sequester themselves in monasteries to minimize the negative influences of physical life and maximize the spiritual. The importance of the physical body was often either put down or rejected in favor of the soul. Strict disciplines were put in place to subordinate the body in hopes of strengthening the "spiritual life" of the believer through contemplation, prayer, and rigorous physical deprivation, sometimes even self-beating or whipping. This idea is more Plato than the apostle Paul.

Since this self-punishment idea doesn't come from

God, it ought not to come from the church, particularly from the pulpit. Sadly, though, we sometimes hear this bad theology from church leaders. It continues to survive in the church in a few different forms—one being that of ascetic pietism. Practically, this means that if it feels good it's bad, and if it feels *really* good it's *really* bad. In this view, all forms of healthy fun or physical pleasure are highly suspect. That's why we need to be careful when we sing such hymns as

> Alas! and did my Savior bleed,
> And did my Sov'reign die?
> Would He devote that sacred head
> For such a worm as I?[3]

The idea that we are unimportant, worthless, too low to count, and insignificant worms amounting to less than a speck in the universe is absolutely not a biblical or Christian idea.

No, we are invited to sing and rejoice because we have great worth and great significance as the beloved creations of the heavenly Father. Whatever God made has value, so we derive our value from him. We are, in the view of the Bible and Christian theology, the "crown of creation" (Genesis 1:26; Psalm 8). It is because we bear God's image and can potentially reflect his glory that we are candidates for sharing the purposes of our glorious

Creator by living in the center of his will. As such, we could wish nothing more or higher for ourselves than submitting to God's perfect will. Trying to fulfill ourselves by ourselves is the formula for failure. Jesus taught that this is an absolute impossibility. He put it this way: "For whoever wants to save their life will lose it, but whoever loses their life for me and for the gospel will save it" (Mark 8:35). And if we put his kingdom first in everything, all the other important things we need and seek for in this life will be given to us (Matthew 6:33).

So the fulfillment of our highest dreams and aspirations lies not in moving God to the back of the bus, or excluding him from our lives while pursuing our own ends, but in putting him in first place and in the driver's seat. Consider what this means for marriage. We have many of our own motives for getting married—love, companionship, sexual desires, longing for children and family, and all the rest. These are good and acceptable things in God's sight. Why wouldn't they be? He made them. Yet he has his own purposes for marriage that transcend all our own and serve as an umbrella over our temporal reasons.

The passage of time teaches us that some of those things that originally caused us to unite with another person for life may mature, fade, or disappear altogether. In a healthy marriage, romantic feelings don't disappear;

instead they deepen and broaden into a more profound love and respect. The companionship should continue to mature, but in some cases, injuries or aging might diminish the mental or emotional capacity to relate to a spouse. Sexuality should continue to satisfy, but accidents, surgeries, and the like can eliminate it earlier in life than expected. Children may or may not continue to accept and love us in later years of development. To put it simply, what got us started may not stay with us forever.

God has reasons and purposes for a marriage that go beyond all such transitory things. True, satisfying, God-ordained marriage is driven by *purpose*. He looks not only at our life span but also at the life spans of generations before and after us that may have never even crossed our minds. Like tossing a pebble into a still pool, everything we do (or fail to do) in this life causes ripples to continue for many years, even centuries. We are the product of such ripples that were caused long before our birth, and we will make our own that can last far beyond us.

My wife and I are married today because of a spontaneous decision made by her great-grandmother half a world away in the late 1800s. Without warning or forethought, she hopped out of a carriage carrying her to a wedding she didn't want. In fear and dread, she fled into the forest. Her family never saw her again. She was found by some British policemen, and after she told them she was lost, they took her to a mission compound where she was taken in and cared for. Later, after she came to faith in Jesus Christ, she was accompanied by missionaries to England to meet Queen Victoria, who was interested in missions. On the ship back to India, she met a young missionary man. Upon arriving in India, he courted and married her. Many, many years later when I interviewed a young, vibrant, beautiful woman applying for a job at my church, I didn't realize that I was meeting my future wife, a fourth-generation Christian with a long family history of faith and ministry. My wife and I believe that God has plans for our marriage and for our two beautiful, godly daughters that will continue to make ripples hundreds of years from now. This is exactly as it should be for a God who sees "the end from the beginning, / [and] from ancient times, what is still to come" (Isaiah 46:10).

What a great relief it is to discover that nothing ever happens by accident in this life! Our higher purpose exists whether we like it or not, whether we believe it or not. It's there. It has always been there. It will be there centuries after our departure. Our eventual acceptance or rejection of it won't have the remotest effect upon its reality. However, it is the recognition of his higher will and our deliberate, happy submission to it that lies at the heart of successful life. Never to know this is one of the greatest and most tragic of life's failures. To bend our knee in honor of the king who rules over us is the beginning of knowledge and wisdom (and joy). It opens the door to all that has value and leads us into the inner rooms of life's meaning.

Many people believe that the key to avoiding disappointment is not to desire things, or at least to desire them less passionately, a thought derived from various philosophies. In the biblical view, it isn't that we desire them with less passion and intensity but that we desire something higher—God's will—with an even greater passion. Jesus desired fervently not to be crucified, but he desired even more greatly to do the will of the Father. When we can say with Job

> The LORD gave and the LORD has taken away;
> may the name of the LORD be praised
> (Job 1:21)

then we'll start to learn what it means to live under the umbrella of the eternal purpose and begin our journey away from blame and anger at God to trust in his better plan for our lives.

If God seems silent to your fervent prayers, or there's no change in your situation, don't give up. It's very common for someone praying for something with all the heart, soul, and faith he or she can muster only to receive either silence from heaven or no change in the situation. For many, this is the last straw and they just throw in the towel, exclaiming, "I've had it. This prayer stuff is worthless!" But what we must keep in mind is that not only does God hear and answer prayer, but he does so in his way and in his time, not ours. He will not be the genie in the bottle. He refuses to become our valet or lieutenant. What he does and when he does it are in his hands and entirely within the framework of his eternal plan and purpose. Our nonnegotiable deadline for the desired answer may be next Tuesday, but God's deadline may be a year from Tuesday or even ten years from Tuesday.

As I discussed in chapter 1 of this book, at the age of twenty-nine I suffered a substantial loss of eyesight. I was barely able to read a single word for seven very long years. During those years I was forced to confront on a daily basis the question of the higher order of things. Was I going to acknowledge that the Lord God was the Ruler of my life, or not? Was I going to continue worshipping and serving him, or was I going to bail out in resentment against his "cruel" will and withhold the honor and glory due him?

Could I worship this God who took away most of what meant anything to me—even the basic requirements and abilities to have a life and career? Could I praise the One who took away as well as gave? These were not easy questions to answer, and the answers didn't come to me quickly. Intense struggle followed, and it didn't end soon.

To make a seven-year-long story much shorter, the answer I finally arrived at was this: God was God and I wasn't. That sounds like a pretty obvious conclusion, but it wasn't at the time. It takes some of us more time than others to come around to the view that there can be only one sovereign in our lives, one captain on the ship. There can't be more than one God in life.

If we decide that first place is to be occupied by our own purpose, then everything else in life will take shape on the basis of this bad decision. But if we understand that only God's purposes can take precedence, then everything else in life will follow suit. As I understand it, God was not under any obligation to solve the problem with my eyesight or anything else. Even though I recognized that truth fairly early on, at least on the intellectual level, it still took more years for me to get that lesson under my belt. The good news is that God has time. He can outwait us!

In the case of Job, he came to the conclusion that God was God, and he didn't necessarily need to explain himself to us or grant some simple, clean-cut answer to our suffering. God should be praised whether he gives or takes away. Ultimately, there may be no easy answer that makes sense of it all, other than the fact that God's purposes go far beyond ours and that in the end we learn that he has our highest good in mind. We may depart from this life without all the answers we wish for, but we may do so with the confidence that they rest in the infinite wisdom of our Creator.

God's kindness throughout our lives points to our final redemption where joy, wholeness, and exquisite pleasure alone are of the highest order. If he could accomplish in us all he wants by giving us good and pleasant things only, he would do so. However, since at the present we don't live in heaven, but in this fallen world, and since by our natures we are given to pursue everything under the sun except the high purposes of God, we will live under this daily training program until graduation day. For God's best and eternal destiny for us, it can't be any other way.

Rebuilding a Theological Foundation

Every time I swallow a watermelon seed, I hear my grandmother's voice warning me that a watermelon will grow inside my stomach. As a kid I thought, *What a terrible thing! How would they ever get it out?* Whenever I saw adults walking around with a large belly, I figured I knew exactly what their problem was—they had a watermelon growing in there!

Some of us still believe things about God that we were taught as children, and this information lingers in the back of our memories long after we've had more factual or better teaching on the subject. We can drag along with us a superstition or some homemade wisdom for much of life, until we learn the truth of a matter and wonder at our foolishness in believing so strongly in something that made no sense whatsoever. In that case, we shouldn't necessarily expect the teaching we first received about God, Jesus, the Bible, or human nature to be much different from what we accepted about eating watermelons. Knowledge about the nature of God, his activity in creating the universe, the coming of his Son in human form, the miracles he performed, his crucifixion and resurrection, what Christian life is like, and what we should do and how we should behave, all are powerfully affected by the first words we were taught about them. Much of this needs to be bulldozed and cleared away before we can start afresh and make any progress in our thinking and faith.

When I started studying theology in a formal way, I found that a great deal of what I had been taught in my early years needed to be put on the back burner or tossed in the trash heap altogether. This was no painless process, for it seemed that my very soul was being destroyed as I tried to do this. Those close to me also thought that I was losing my faith and were very concerned. In a sense, I *was* losing my faith; but the earliest forms of it were being transformed or replaced with something better. The essence of my faith—trust in God—was preserved intact, but the superstructure, or the theological house sitting on the foundation, was being renovated. Like most construction sites, it wasn't pretty.

In truth, our thinking about God ought always to be in the process of being reevaluated and refined. We need to be renovating our theological houses continually. By this, I don't mean we should always be starting from scratch or attempting to wed the world's philosophies with Christian faith. We need to keep the basics of faith and stay centered on the Bible but also continue to find better ways of understanding and communicating the good news. Once we stop doing that, we stop growing.

I can't stress enough the importance of staying in Scripture throughout our lives because we learn fresh insights with each new stage of our growth. As we move from one level of development to another, we read the Bible with new lenses and learn something new. And if we stop growing theologically in our younger years, we will then take the thoughts and perceptions of a novice into our adult life. This creates a huge problem because our childhood insight into the Bible determines our adult understanding of it. Just like the watermelon seeds and the crossed eyes, it's all too easy to misread the Bible through the lenses of what Grandma or Uncle Frank once said about it or even through what we saw with our adolescent eyes.

When we mature we compare our adolescent, naïve understanding of Christian faith with the highly developed intellect of an adult regarding every other department of life (philosophy, sociology, the physical sciences, history, or just plain daily living), and faith always comes up short. It will invariably seem too childish and simple. That's because it is! We're not intended to let our childhood comprehension of the most important reality of life (God) carry us through life. It's like trying to wear the same sweater you wore when you were ten. As we advance in our understanding of life on every other level, we're expected to match this stride for stride with our faith. Like a secondhand faith, a thoughtless or underdeveloped faith is worthless.

The only antidote to this lopsided development is to keep the Bible in front of us. The common testimony of the believer is to look up from the Bible reading of the day and say, "I've been reading this book for years, but I've never seen that verse until this morning. It's as if it had been written during the night just for me!"

So the Bible remains the foundation of our thinking, not only about God, but also about every topic it touches upon. It informs our views on human nature, the meaning of history, how we are to treat one another, what we are to believe about morals and ethics, and so forth. It doesn't mean that it's easy reading or that there are no problems with its interpretation (the Bible contains some of the most difficult literature ever written). It means that we're to apply it wherever and as often as it speaks to our situation. Also, it's good to study it in a community of believers. We can help one another understand it by pointing out one another's blind spots (we all have them), and a family of interpreters is often better than just one.

When listening to preachers and teachers, we can compare their thoughts with the thoughts of others we already trust and then decide if certain speakers are worth listening to. Just because "God spoke to them" or they have their Bible draped over their hands as they speak, it doesn't necessarily mean a thing. Today a virtual army of self-proclaimed "Bible experts" or "prophets" (God "told" them to declare their opinions and share their feelings) has been set loose on the unsuspecting world. But not every one of them should be believed just because they attract huge crowds and have their own television slots on Sunday mornings. I've listened to a great number of these preachers and teachers and have found that while some have helpful messages to bring us, and we can profit by listening to them, many (if not most) preach the same messages I heard from my Grandma or Uncle Frank years ago—before I knew anything about the Bible or theology.

The first-century church was very careful to distinguish the real teachers from the fake ones. The apostle Paul told his churches that if anyone came preaching a message other than the one they all received from the beginning, then let that preacher go to hell (Galatians 1:8). Paul didn't mince words! In the English translations, the language has been smoothed out a bit to make it sound a little nicer in church. We don't think that's a very appropriate thing for a spiritual leader to say, but it's what he said and it's what he meant. Believers were exhorted not even to let a teacher in the door unless he brought with him the right message (2 John 10).

If you're getting a gospel that doesn't look and sound like the original, it should be tossed out. The reason all this is so important is that the message contains the description of the God of all things, the Ruler of the universe, and the King of kings. When the message is wrong, it unloads upon us a lesser god, a deity who brings not the good news (the meaning of the word *gospel*) but mere religion (the bad news) with its rules, rituals, manipulation, guilt, and bondage.

When I was a teen, I received some pretty "bad news" messages. I had been invited to go see a movie, but here was my dilemma. Knowing that going to a movie was frowned upon and considered a very bad thing in my church, I asked one of the leading Christian teachers in my circle what would happen if Jesus Christ returned to the earth and brought history to a close at the very moment I was sitting in a movie theater. Would that disqualify me from going to heaven? He looked down at the ground for a moment, shook his head slightly from side to side, and in a deep, grave voice said, "Well...we just don't know." I didn't go to the movies.

On another occasion, when I was contemplating whether or not to attend a school dance (dancing was also high on the forbidden list), I asked a Christian neighbor what God might think of it. He said he'd be happy to help me. In fact, he had a book at home that would clear the confusion and indecision. Soon after, he produced a little pamphlet entitled *From the Ballroom to Hell*. Needless to say, I didn't go to the prom either.

Years later, I was sharing these stories with a missionary friend and found out that he had had a much worse experience. He decided to go and see a much-talked-about, epic film. When his deacons heard about this, they got together and decided to fire him from his church. The film? Cecil B. DeMille's *The Ten Commandments*.

Now try to imagine what kind of deity we're talking about here. Any "god" who would exclude people from his kingdom and send them into eternal separation and destruction for sitting in a theater watching a film or going to a dance would be too frightening to be around. Would you ever want to have anything to do with this being? What kind of salvation message would this be? Is salvation something so slippery to hold on to that if we're not careful it could, in scant moments, slip through our fingers like sand? Is this sort of do-it-yourself salvation what the Bible proclaims to us? The answer is an obvious no. No way!

This understanding of God is merely a modern version of a very ancient heresy. Much the same thing was expressed by one of the second-century Church Fathers, Athenagoras, who declared in his treatise Athenagoras' Plea that if during a worship gathering the slightest bad or lustful thought happened to pass through a Christian's mind while passing the kiss of peace (a religious salutation), then the person would automatically forfeit eternal life.[4] One random thought at the wrong moment and he buys a one-way ticket to hell. What an appalling and frightening view of our Creator! No, this type of "gospel" and this kind of "god" is light-years from what we read about in the Bible. You may have your own ideas about dancing and films, but that has nothing to do with the gospel. The advice I received from my devout, religious leader and from my neighbor was not just a variation of the gospel; it was no gospel at all but a complete renunciation of the original good news.

For peddling such a false message, Paul would have said, "Put him on the first train out of town!" or, more likely, something much worse. Yet millions of unsuspecting people have grotesque distortions of God unloaded on them daily, particularly every Sunday, either from their home churches, on the computer, on television, or from a well-meaning friend. The wrong ideas we hear about God will create a view of life so far from reality that this deity would be impossible to love or serve. The poor recipient will eventually either discard such a being altogether or try desperately to live up to impossible expectations in constant fear of condemnation. Both avenues are dead ends. One will mean that the real God will be tossed out with the false. The other will result in falling short of the standard every day and in every way (with plenty of frustration and guilt) or living with the delusion that one is doing quite well in keeping the rules of the game. This latter outcome would cause a person to end up an insufferable, self-righteous fuddy-duddy, full of resentment toward God and without the slightest idea about divine grace and mercy. That is not what the gospel of Jesus Christ teaches us.

What Jesus Teaches Us

Jesus neutralizes false faith by giving us the truth. The real God, our heavenly Father, realizes that we can't—that we are wholly unable to—fulfill the requirements of salvation by our own efforts. Forgiveness and salvation are gifts that he gives us free of charge (because Jesus paid the price for us) and are to be received with the simplicity of a child. We can't barter with God for them. We can't trade any of our own merits for them. We can't substitute our own efforts at being good, nice, or religious. We can't make it better by anything we do or say. We can only want it, reach out, and gratefully receive it from the open hand of our God. Any and all attempts to be good enough, to act "spiritual" enough, to keep the rules well enough (such as avoiding going to movies and all the rest of the foolish things that inept religious leaders warn against), will not have the slightest effect upon our relationship with God.

Since it's God through Jesus his Son who comes to us first with his hands open, who first thinks of us as being part of his family, and who initiates our adoption into his family (Ephesians 1:3-6), it's his Son alone who keeps us throughout life from falling and finally presents us "without fault and with great joy" at the end (Jude 24).

One of the recurring themes of this book is to point out the extent to which our picture of God's character and purposes determines the level of our resentment toward him and how much we blame him. Here is one of those critical points we need to plant firmly in our minds: God is never *less* than we imagine him to be but always *more*. He is never less forgiving, less loving, less faithful, less patient, but always just as he is portrayed in Scripture. When he is severe toward his people, it is for their redemption. When he corrects and disciplines his children, it is for their good (Proverbs 3:11-12; Hebrews 12:10).

When he brings judgment to them, it is to put right side up that which is upside down. It is the consistent teaching of Jesus that God comes to us with more grace than we would expect, and more than we would recommend. His grace is granted outrageously and in excessively large doses to many of those we would imagine (or even wish) to be completely outside the realm of his acceptance.

His grace and mercy are so extreme that when the true gospel is declared, it's inevitable that it will be misinterpreted by many of its hearers as libertinism (too much freedom) or antinomianism (too little law). The true gospel operates just inches from the edge of heresy. It will always sound to the legalist (the rule keeper) as too generous, too free, or too merciful.

No matter how long you once lived outside the family of God, how many times you've violated the laws of God, or for how long a period of time, God is still a God of grace and forgiveness. If you think you've gone too far over the edge to receive reconciliation and new life, don't! Your misunderstanding will only lead to a more distorted and twisted view of God and his supposed unwillingness to restore and rescue. Despair in trying to measure up will set in when you presume that God is too righteous or too holy to forgive you, and then resentment will inevitably follow. Such thinking is far from what we read in the pages of the New Testament, which affirms that God is just as near to the person who has sinned flagrantly for decades as he is to the one who seemingly has done very little wrong in comparison (Luke 23:39-43).

It is still God in his mercy who, in the language of theology, both *imputes* and *imparts*. First he *imputes*, or credits, us with the righteousness of Jesus his Son. He sees us through the lenses of Jesus's purity. He looks upon us as if we were just as perfect as his perfect Son. We know we aren't, and he knows we aren't, but in his love for us and in his desire to save and heal, he puts the perfect record of his Son to our credit as we stand under the shadow of Jesus's protection.

Let's consider this in another way. A convicted felon is standing before the judge, totally guilty of the crime of which he's accused. All the evidence is in, and the jury, completely convinced of the man's culpability, took only a few minutes to deliberate. The evidence was overwhelming and decisive, and when asked for their verdict, they reply, "Guilty on all counts." After hearing this, the judge then says, "I know that a guilty verdict is the only possibility here, but I'm going to pronounce this person 'not guilty' because the court desires to show mercy. I will pay the price for his law-breaking so this defendant is now free to go. All accusations have been expunged from his record and he is now completely pardoned and absolved of all crimes. His violations of the law are not even to be mentioned ever again." But that's not the end of it. The judge not only *imputes* to the guilty man the status of "pardoned" and "absolved of all crimes" but also begins to meet privately with the freed criminal in order to influence him to lead a law-abiding and productive life. He's not satisfied with just pardoning him. He wants to see him change into someone who loves to live in harmony with the laws of the land and truly desires to be a contributing member of society. In other words, the judge wants not only to *impute* to him the rightness that he doesn't really possess but also to *impart* to him the rightness that he needs to live well in the community. He wants him to be a good citizen who enjoys obeying the just laws and to become the kind of person who doesn't want to commit crimes any longer.

I know the parallels I've suggested aren't perfect. There aren't any perfect analogies since only God does this. It's unique. But this example, hopefully, clarifies a little more what is meant when it's said that God offers us his mercy and free grace. He finds us where we are, just as we are, and then chooses to have mercy upon us just because it's his good pleasure to do so. Then he comes to dwell with and within us and by his Spirit to *impart* some of his character, so that over time we'll become the kind of people he wants us to be.

The good news is that all of this has absolutely nothing

to do with how much evil we've contributed to the world or for how long we've sinned. It is related only to the level of mercy God chooses to send our way. It is based wholly upon *his* character not *ours*. The more we've failed and violated his will, the more grace he *imparts* to us. The farther we've drifted from him, the longer and stronger the lifeline needs to be. Now stop and think about this incredible fact. Who else does this? Which of the world's belief systems even comes close to presenting this kind of Being? So the greater our life of disobedience and foolishness, the more grateful we'll be for his mercy. That is why some of the brightest shining lights in the family of faith have been in their past some of the lowest and worst specimens of depraved humanity ever to crawl out from under a rock. God saves people, not because they're good, but because they're not.

The New Testament is full of such illustrations. The criminal on the cross next to Jesus says, "Don't forget me!" Jesus responds with something like, "That's good enough for me—I'll see you in paradise this afternoon" (my paraphrase of Luke 23:39-43). The woman with a checkered past sheds tears on Jesus's feet, and he grants her a free ticket into his eternal kingdom (Luke 7:36-48). It seemed that Jesus just couldn't wait to hand out these free passes to anyone who wanted them, no matter how low and undeserving. That is grace. The Pharisees around him perceived such "irresponsible" behavior as the height of audacity (they called him "raving mad"), and it got him into enough trouble to get him nailed to a cross.

When we find ourselves becoming resentful toward God or blaming him for one reason or another, we need to return to the Scriptures and learn again what kind of God we're resenting. Is this the one true God, or have we managed to allow some other portrayal to twist our perception of him? Remember that one of Satan's favorite activities is to slander God and create distortions in our minds about him.

The obvious way to rid our minds of wrong ideas is to displace them with right ones. What this requires in practical terms is to read the Bible consistently. If we don't follow this exercise, we can be absolutely sure that false ideas will find room in our thinking. If we continually allow ourselves to be informed by the falseness around us, we won't recognize the Father of whom Jesus speaks. A lot of the time, this may not be intentional. We're not actively rejecting God. We're attending church, saying our prayers, and thanking him for his blessings. But suppose for a moment we're living in an environment of comfort and pleasure in one of *Forbes'* top-ten cities to enjoy your best life. Things are going great, but everyone around us has a laissez-faire attitude toward God. By osmosis, we could easily become one of them. Soon, we're buying into the god of their creation and then angry that he's not delivering on our expectations.

Most resentment has, at its foundation, a wrong deity in mind. More often than not, if we delve back into the Bible, we'll recognize the deity we resent has little to do with the God revealed to us in the scriptures. If false and distorted views have been building up in our thinking over a period of months or even years, it's time to wash them out with the pure mountain water of truth. Even for those who preach the gospel, it is regularly declaring the truth of Jesus that keeps them from despair and doubts of their own.

Remember our earlier discussion of Martin Luther in chapter 2? For him, God had seemed a demanding, unaffectionate, cold-blooded, tyrannical figure who took no prisoners when it came to the perfect performance of his will. If you obeyed the rules, then things tended to work out. If you didn't (or couldn't), then things went very badly for you. In Luther's case, he found that he couldn't manage to fulfill the demands of God no matter how hard he tried. It was only several years of studying the Bible that led him to see clearly for the first time the God who had been obscured and distorted by the religious establishment, its human traditions, and its leaders, very much as had been done in Jesus's day.

When Luther emerged from the long tunnel of doubt

and fear, from the darkness of false ideas about God and his good purposes, he sounded a bell that was heard throughout Europe. This highly personal change brought about a revolution on an entire continent. All he intended to do was to restore the original gospel of Jesus to the church he loved. He wanted everyone to enjoy the God he had come to discover—the Mighty Fortress, the Bulwark never failing, the God whom Jesus preached, the Giver of gifts, the Father who couldn't wait to lavish his mercy and grace upon the most undeserving. This God was so astonishingly new and surprising because he was so unlike everything Luther had ever learned.

Is the Creator the unreasonable tyrant who can't be pleased? Is he the impatient, unyielding, and immovable rule-giver who makes no effort to lift the burdens of those who labor under him? God is neither of these. He is the heavenly Father who, as the psalmist David said, does not deal with us according to our sins or pay us back for our transgressions (Psalm 103:10). We get the good we don't deserve, and we don't get the bad we do deserve. It's God's first preference not to judge and punish his people but to love and honor them. When there is judgment upon them, it's primarily out of a desire to redirect or rescue them through loving, parental discipline. This is what Jesus taught us about God.

Chapter 7

LIVING IN A REDEMPTION STORY

When we have a correct view of God and are living under truthful teaching, with God's help we can structure our lives around the divine purpose to live each and every day with God at the center and his will as our guide. How do we do this? By regularly reading the Scriptures and staying in prayer for specific and personal instructions on a day-to-day basis.

Often God is simply waiting for our deliberate submission to his will before blessing us lavishly. I once knew a pastor in California who was serving in a church where he was in line to take the senior pastor's position when he retired. However, instead of being promoted, he was summarily fired. Without any other way of making a living for his family, he ended up working for a large supermarket chain. He spent his days mostly hosing down the huge garbage bins in the back parking lot.

One day, as he was washing the last banana peel off the side of the dumpster, he felt that God was speaking to him. Within his heart, God posed this question to him: "If this is the best that you'll ever do in life, are you willing to serve and love me right here, till the end of your days?" This was not a question he could quickly or easily answer. For many days he struggled with this enormous life issue. "Could I praise God washing garbage cans in the parking lot of this market for the rest of my life? Will I love and serve him even if I never make it in the eyes of the world or the church?"

It was only after an extended time of deep and serious reflection and wrestling within his spirit that he reached the point where he was able to say, "Yes, even if I have to spend my entire life in this place doing nothing but cleaning oversized trash cans, I'll serve God just because he's the Sovereign Lord. I'll praise him just because he's worthy to be praised. Yes, I can and will do that."

Soon after this sincere confession of obedience and submission, he was called to a new church. It grew so quickly that the congregation soon exceeded the size of the building. In search of a large enough facility, he ran across the only place in the city sufficient to do the job—a closed-down, boarded-up supermarket of the same chain! That place was his church until his death. God has not only a sense for justice and mercy but a flair for the dramatic and a healthy sense of humor as well.

Embracing Repentance

Learning to live in the story God has written for each of us requires facing our hurts and resentments against God and bringing them into the light. In order to begin to move out of resentment, we first have to pass through the door of repentance. Repentance means that we have the God-given privilege and gift, at any point in life, of starting over or returning to the place where we first drifted off our God-ordained path. Repentance is something that God *grants* us (2 Timothy 2:25). We are given the chance to stop and apologize to God for offending him and tarnishing his reputation with our lives and to ask for a renewed relationship with him. The first step is to confess that he alone is sovereign and that he alone is the Director of our lives. He is ever ready to forgive us our sins and cleanse us from all the stains caused by our recklessness and foolishness, or our peevishness and resentment.

Repentance is usually tough for us—even a virtual impossibility. We can find it difficult to use the *r* word. Why is repentance so hard? It is beyond our puny efforts and can't be done without some supernatural power to help us. But that's exactly what God offers us. We're guaranteed that the force that brought the universe into being is the same force that will swoop down and set us free from our radical self-worship and chronic, addictive, all-consuming self-dependence.

Here's the good news: we can always start anew with God. Let's look again at the parable of the Prodigal Son, or closer to the meaning of the story, the parable of the Waiting Father (Luke 15:11-31). As the story goes, a young man demands his share of his inheritance from his father. Amazingly, the father actually grants him his wish. The son heads off, pockets full, to the far country in search of excitement and adventure. Eventually, he runs out of steam and finds himself without friends, without fun, and without funds. He remembers the good days of plenty with his father.

He reasons to himself that he'd be infinitely better off as a hired hand on the family ranch than where he is, working on a pig farm in some hostile foreign land. He rehearses the apology he's going to give to his father when he returns home: "Father, I have sinned against heaven and against you. I am no longer worthy to be called your son" (Luke 15:21). He's hoping to receive at least a small amount of understanding, not to mention a little room and board. His expectations are minimal. But what happens to him next is totally unexpected.

As the son draws near his home, the father is waiting for him—longingly. He sees the son at a distance, but instead of waiting for him to move slowly toward home and letting him grovel for a while before granting him a chilly reception and a menial job, the father leaps up from his place and with reckless abandon sprints across the field. Before his son has a chance to try out his well-rehearsed apology, he's quickly embraced, kissed, and given a royal welcome—the best robe, a ring of honor, and a great feast in celebration of his return. The son is lavished with the father's forgiveness and affection.

We have the same privilege offered to us *right now*. When we become weary of living in the pigsty of human rebellion and folly, we can return home to our Father's house just like the rebellious son. We can expect that he'll be looking through the window with the same antici-pation as the prodigal's father. We can receive the same warm welcome home and extravagant celebration that the son received. We can start all over again and live the life we always should have lived but failed to. It has been said that, with God, it's never too late to become what you could have been. It doesn't matter how old you are or how many days you have left on this earth; it's never too late to return home to our loving Father.

Through repentance, we can structure our lives around the divine purpose. We can say farewell to the wasted years of wilderness wandering and welcome the entrance of God's plan. We can repent in prayer or in song. One of the greatest songs of repentance ever writ-ten is that by Johann Franck and Johann Sebastian Bach,

"Jesus, My Joy." It has become the favorite of many people over the centuries as an expression of the futility of life lived outside of the divine will and the relief of saying good-bye to it. Read carefully the inspired words, and if they apply, even pray them yourself, making them your own. Others have done so before you:

Verse 1
Jesus, priceless treasure,
source of purest pleasure,
friend most sure and true:
long my heart was burning,
fainting much and yearning,
thirsting, Lord, for you.
Yours I am, O spotless Lamb,
so will I let nothing hide you,
seek no joy beside you!

Verse 2
Let your arms enfold me:
those who try to wound me
cannot reach me here.
Though the earth be shaking,
every heart be quaking,
Jesus calms my fear.
Fires may flash and thunder crash;
yea, though sin and hell assail me,
Jesus will not fail me.

Verse 4
Banish thoughts of sadness,
for the Lord of gladness,
Jesus, enters in;
though the clouds may gather,
those who love the Savior
still have peace within.
Though I bear much sorrow here,
still in you lies purest pleasure,
Jesus, priceless treasure![1]

Once you have repented, we can regard all the confusions and delusions that entered our lives and threw us off track as mere building blocks to faith. God is able and willing to take all those days, years, or even decades of futility and failure and transform them into valuable learning experiences. We can see them as trials through which we've grown. This isn't to say that they were good things or that they were somehow virtues masquerading as vices. We need to own up to and call them what they really were—sin, folly, vice, stupidity, pride, foolishness. For some people, it's an enormous relief just to be so absolutely, bluntly honest about themselves.

The way God brings about change in us is through conviction, confession, repentance, and restoration. By the enlightenment of the Holy Spirit, we come to recognize that we're on the wrong course—we are wrong and

God is right. That is conviction. By confession, we admit fully and express clearly that we were wrong. No excuses. It was our fault, not somebody else's. We maturely take full responsibility and accept the blame for our actions. In repentance, we willingly turn from our wrong course and, with God's help, deliberately head in the new direction.

God is the divine alchemist who can transform one thing into another. With just a simple creative word, he can speak life into your situation of death. He can take the raw material of your sins, shame, or suffering and turn them into the building materials of your recovery. Only he can do this. We can't. Only he can create something out of nothing, or something good and useful out of something bad and destructive. He can and will do it. It's one of his favorite things to do!

Such dramatic and creative rescues have been God's purpose from the very beginning of the world. The first chapter of Genesis describes a wonderful image of the work of God's Spirit. The writer portrays the Spirit of God hovering over the unformed and unruly mass of disorder and chaos. He then extracts out of this chaos wondrous order and purpose. This great work of bringing harmony and order out of tangled clutter becomes the job description of the Holy Spirit for the remainder of world history.

His Spirit continues to hover over our disarrayed

lives to invade, occupy, transform, and create out of our confused and jumbled existence a glorious pattern. This doesn't happen automatically or just because we want it to. It happens when we come home to our Father, when we approach our Creator in humility and repentance, confessing our complicity in the hostility and rebellion that rule our world.

Lavish forgiveness is available, but it comes with our open admission for the need. Ironically, in this, our most dreaded of all personal experiences, lies the key to ongoing happiness. We would rather do anything than face up to it and admit that all of our perceptions were wrong. Yet when it's over, we realize that the pain was usually less than we expected, and the result is incomparably superior to our original condition.

After the spiritual disciplines of confession and repentance become a regular part of our lives, they become easier, for with each new experience we realize a greater level of health and joy than before. That's the way God made things. The simple words, "I'm sorry, I was wrong, please forgive me," may be intensely hard in the beginning for some of us to say, but if meant, these words have the power to fix marriages, restore alienated friendships, and patch up broken business relationships and every other personal connection we develop in life. When God hears them, he doesn't say, "Well, it's about time you came crawling back to me." Rather, he simply gives us a smile and a warm welcome home.

For those who aren't there yet, who are still angry and resentful, the waiting Father is still waiting. For some it takes more time than others. But remember, every minute you spend in this condition you will eventually look back upon as wasted time. The desire to repent *is* repentance. The desire to come home is the first step in getting there. If you've drifted off course through a season of resentment, blame, and bitterness toward God, there is a way back. If you'd like to begin making the change right now but aren't sure how to take the first step, you could pray something like this:

> *Lord, I'm sorry for trying to play God and not acknowledging—or for ignoring—your authority over my life. I regret all the wasted efforts of my life. I want you to forgive me for all that I've done to offend you, bring dishonor to your name, stain your reputation, or diminish your glory. Bring me back to the place where you alone are Lord and I'm your willing subject. Give me a new start and renew my lost friendship with you. Put a new and right spirit within me, for Jesus's sake. Amen.*

Seeing the Bigger Picture

The good news is that God has reserved the most dramatic, wonderful, over-the-top resolution for the darkest and most depressing aspects of life's sorrows and disappointments, such as loss, disappointment, aging, and death. Our society finds life's slow march toward the end, and all that it entails along the way, so grim that it does everything in its power to avoid even thinking about it. According to a recent study, the anti-aging market size and trends will reach $216.52 billion by 2021.[2] Translated, this means billions of dollars are spent each year on products designed to cover or slow down the aging process, to help us pretend it doesn't exist, or to enable us to put the evidence of it far out of sight.

Acres of land have been transformed into such beautiful lush gardens and parks, we scarcely recognize them for what they are—graveyards. In generations past, carefully etched tombstones in churchyards reminded us in the clearest possible way that this is the future place of residence for our earthly bodies. These visual realities kept us somewhat humble and aware of the light hold we have on this passing world.

Although today's graveyards are usually kept out of view, they still serve as a harsh reminder of our own mortality and the mortality of those we love. I know of professed, hardboiled deniers of God who became that way when they lost someone of great value to them—a friend, a brother or sister, a parent, or a child. Many people have walked away from God the moment they walked out of the funeral home. When all the philosophical arguments and objections to the Bible are peeled away, often the death of a loved one, or some other shattering personal loss or discouragement, lies at the center of our resentment and rejection of God.

But it is precisely in death where God attacks head-on and defeats all human struggles. It is here where the heart of the Christian hope lies and where our resentment finds its real and all-encompassing resolution. There would have been no Christian faith, no New Testament, and no hope for anyone if Jesus hadn't been raised from the dead and promised that this same resurrection would be the destiny of his followers. It's the resurrection of Jesus, and that alone, that forms the bedrock for the entire edifice that we call the Christian faith.

In Romans 8:18-25 and 1 Corinthians 15 the apostle Paul wrote one of the most extravagant accounts of what the future holds for those who are part of God's family. He begins by word painting a vast panorama of salvation, including not merely human beings, but all of creation, the entire universe and all that's in it. He portrays the earth and everything else that God originally made as the objects of his eternal rescue and restoration. Not a single good thing will be forgotten or overlooked, and not a single bad thing will even be remembered. God will rescue the entire physical realm.

Against this backdrop, Paul speaks of what our personal histories mean in the light of all this good news. We are not merely meaningless mistakes who just happened by chance to be on this planet. We are here by design and will leave only by divine appointment. In the meantime, a thoughtful and purposeful (and loving) Ruler permits all that happens to us in this life—everything without exception.

To those who love God, who are called according to his purpose, absolutely nothing will happen that will not in some way be used for good (Romans 8:28). Whose good? God's good, of course! But if it's only for God's good, then what benefit is that to us? As Paul would say, "Much, in every way!" If it's good for God, then it can't be bad for us.

All this talk about the redemption of the physical universe was a great shock, even an annoyance, to many of the pagan philosophers and theologians of the apostle Paul's day. They believed that only the immaterial "soul" was important. The rest of the entire physical world was relatively unimportant, a more or less temporary inconvenience. Even the Jewish thinkers of Paul's day, who believed that the material world was valuable and meaningful (because God created it), still didn't possess a clearly worked out picture of what would actually happen to it at the end of history. Things were a bit fuzzy. There were hints here and there of some sort of restoration of all things in the final wrap-up of history, but nothing so spectacular as what the apostle lays out for us in Romans.

No one in the ancient world would have wasted a moment on Jesus's claims if it hadn't been for the rock-solid conviction that he had been raised on Easter morning, that he ever lives to help his people on the earth, and that everyone who follows him will emerge victoriously from death's grip. Through his resurrection and ascension he is always present and forever lives to help us fulfill our God-given purpose on earth. We need to grasp the importance of resurrection life and what it implies for us both in this life as well as in the next. If we don't know what to hope for tomorrow, we won't know how to live today. If we miss this point, we've missed everything the gospel has to say.

When asked, most Christians have conflicting opinions of what the resurrection of Jesus means. Often, these explanations bear no resemblance to the facts. When the Gospels state that Jesus arose from the dead, they don't imply that he abandoned the physical world or that we will too. It was clearly not a "spiritual resurrection" where the so-called "Christ Spirit" emerged from the tomb, leaving the body of Jesus to decay. No, his body rose as well, and that was purposeful. Raised on the ideas of the Old Testament, Jewish people wanted absolutely nothing to do with ghosts (spirits without bodies) or corpses (bodies without spirits). For them, to be fully and truly human was to have both body and soul together in one unitary whole.

This was why the New Testament writers specifically testified (they made a huge deal about it!) that when Jesus was raised from death, he appeared in a physical body to his disciples (and to some of his skeptics), even retaining the marks of his recent crucifixion. His body was a transformed body to be sure. It could do things that his pre-resurrection body apparently did not, but it was a body at least as physical as it had always been. Jesus graphically demonstrated this physicality by eating fish in front of his disciples and even invited Thomas to reach out and touch him, so that they could allay their doubts and not think the whole thing was merely an illusion or hallucination.

Jesus certified his resurrection, Luke tells us, with many irrefutable proofs over a period of nearly six weeks (Acts 1:3). In other words, he fulfilled every form of proof anyone needed or wanted in order to be convinced beyond a shadow of a doubt that he was very much alive in a physical body. This fact is doubly important for us because the body that Jesus demonstrated to his disciples is the kind of body we're told we'll have one day. According to the apostle Paul, the resurrection body of Jesus is the model of our resurrection body (1 Corinthians 15:49). It illustrates the quality of life that all those who follow Jesus will enjoy as their final destiny, transformed by him for eternal life in his real, physical kingdom.

If we take seriously the entire biblical witness regarding our future, we are free to turn loose our imaginations to envision it. This life is to be lived on a recreated, transformed physical earth, very much like this present one. We may envision trees, lakes, waterfalls, rivers, animals, mountains and rocks, fields and flowers, great gardens, food, pleasure, adventure, learning, love, and all the rest. God's redemption is for everything he has made—all creation (Romans 8:18-23). The main difference (and our enormous takeaway) is that there will be no evil there, no rebellion against God, no selfishness, accidents, sadness, depression, hatred, resentment, deception, murder, violence, terrorism, war, or death. Words such as *cancer*, *osteoporosis*, *Alzheimer's*, *PTSD*, *tetra-amelia syndrome*, *Parkinson's*, and others won't even be in the dictionary. There will be none of the evil, nor even the possibility of it, that characterizes life on earth now. Pleasure and joy will be the chief order of business. Not only will resentment be obsolete but also every cause of it won't even exist!

Skeptics consider all this just blue sky and roses, wishful thinking, something too good to be true—a crutch. Maybe you're thinking the same thing right now as you read this. But both the Old and New Testaments testify that this is the kind of life God promises to us. I'm spending time on this issue because it's the centerpiece of God's solution to all our earthly problems. So bear with me. Consider a few things and you'll see that what I've outlined is not just fantasy or delusion. It's the most logical and reasonable thing one should expect, given some basic information about God and his created order.

In our journey toward healing, we've seen that a great deal of our resentment against God stems from our complete misperception of him and his purposes. But when we understand what kind of God set this whole thing in motion in the first place, we'll begin to see that what the New Testament promises as our destiny is not at all impossible to believe or too good to be true. Let's start by reviewing some facts.

First, we were created for joy. We were designed and wired for a life of pleasure and joy and definitely *not* intended to live under the stresses and strains of what we call "real life." All the miseries of this world—the sorrows, depressions, pains, disappointments, hatred, resentments, frustrations, the blaming, and all the rest—are not our natural, God-intended environment. As mentioned earlier, this is fairly easily demonstrated by the fact that terrible emotions can make us sick, but their opposites make us well. We break down under the one and heal under the other. No one ever got sick and needed psychotherapy from experiencing too much joy! Nor does one think about going to the doctor because he or she is happy. Yet many are sick and dying both emotionally and physically because of the lack of joy and happiness in their lives. So we may assume that our natural, intended state of being is simply lightheartedness.

Second, no one can possibly miss the fact that the world has gone very wrong. Wherever we look, at any culture we choose to examine, there seems to be a huge flaw at the center. Where is the simple justice we expect for everyone or the basic courtesies and respect that we all seem to require? What accounts for the massive squalor and deprivation we see around the planet? And why do we know deep down inside that "this shouldn't be happening," or "this simply isn't right"? We could say that these expectations are just relative to the culture ("the way we've been socialized"), but it's not difficult to prove that every culture that ever existed had some basic rules and expectations built into it that sound very much like the Old Testament's Ten Commandments.[3]

However we choose to slice it, things remain much the same for all the people of the world. We want a life that we don't have. We imagine the good things that aren't there. We hope for a future that's better than the present. We're convinced that somewhere out there is a reality higher than what we're now experiencing. It seems that God has imprinted upon our minds and consciences the image of heaven, even if we've never had a glimpse of it here on earth. If one nation has more of the good things than another, then the citizens of the one will hope and try for a move to the better. We all seem to be seeking a paradise we can't see in the place where we now are.

In spite of the radically different religions of the world, most of them envision something better than what we see now. The vast majority of the earth's population is convinced that there's something real after this present, earthly life. Not all of them look to a personal God for these benefits, but they do try to picture a higher state, a higher consciousness, and a higher level of existence than the present. They're convinced that the present decaying world, without something better somewhere, is just too *bad* to be true. They're right. Through these longings built into us, if we're paying attention, God informs us in a kaleidoscope of ways that our future is brilliant. In Jesus Christ, God has given us a genuine, solid reason to hope for the best. Only through Christ's resurrection (as the fulfillment of Old Testament anticipations) is there any hope for something better beyond.

Think hard about the question we all ask: can God create a paradise for us? He's already done it once. It's called planet Earth. There was a time when it didn't exist. It came from nothing. Now it's something. Just take a walk outside and look all around you. Sure, it's fairly well corrupted or polluted in many ways, but it's still there. If it weren't right in front of us every day of the week, then it would be very hard to believe that it could ever exist. It would sound like a fairy tale if someone were to claim that it would appear some day in the future. But it does exist, a vast wonderland for all physical life. What we're expected to believe is that what God did once, he can do again. How hard is that to believe? At the end of the day, we may admit that future life is no more improbable than the present one.

Where does all this theology lead us? It means that whatever we may experience in this life, we can get through it if we look beyond to the surety and joy of what is to come (Revelation 21:1-4). The New Testament writers repeatedly tell us that the glories of the future hope far outweigh the pains and sorrows (and resentments) of the present. When we know the outcome of something, it makes it much easier to endure the long haul of difficulty.

It's much the same with the knowledge of God's future plans for us. We can keep going because, if we follow God's plan, we are guaranteed a happily-ever-after ending. This means that we press on and through it all, not just marking time waiting for the end, but moved by energy and enthusiasm, doing good, before the end comes. Our confidence in God's paradise at the end is high motivation and great excitement for doing his will between now and then.

Recognizing Resurrection in the Here and Now

If, and when, we come to recognize our future destiny for what it is (and isn't), then we're in a position to understand the nature of our life lived now, with all its ups and downs, before all this is eventually realized. Resurrection has enormous implications for earthly human life long before we actually reach the end.

Fortunately, resurrection power operates in our midst in ways we usually don't even recognize at first glance. It has influences upon even the tiny details of our daily existence. Far from being the remote and unbelievable theological oddity it's often thought to be, it lies at the very center of the most mundane things. So then let's take a closer look at how resurrection affects our lives and how it helps us with the process of dumping our resentments and anger.

If this book were primarily about the implications of resurrection for human life and society, I would want to emphasize that it validates the great importance of physical life, the material world, and history. This is far more significant than we might expect, and many ancient philosophers and heretics were not on board with this idea. I would also have to include many modern Christians who are looking forward to leaving the physical world behind once and for all. The New Testament stands firmly against this view.

Jesus's resurrection assures us that we're not left alone to pull ourselves out of the hole. We're not destitute on some remote island and left to our own devices. Rescue is available in the here and now. The reality that Jesus was brought back from the dead in a real, physical body, to demonstrate what kind of life we can live in the future, tells us a lot about what kinds of things we can hope to experience long before we leave this world.

The certainty that, through Jesus, God defeated death for all time affirms this one life-transforming fact: whatever situation in which we may find ourselves now, no matter how desperate or loathsome, it can't be all that bad, since the worst has already been conquered. This is where the issue of blame and resentment finds its ultimate resolution. Most resentment against God develops through the illusion that he doesn't care or because we think he took from us something of great value that we can't ever get back.

Some of the biggest losses we experience in life are of

things we can't recover through our own efforts or ingenuity. We don't have the power or the wisdom to restore them or to bring back to life what has taken the one-way road of death. It is here, through Christ, where we can hop off the merry-go-round of bitterness and alienation from God. Let's say you've suffered some long season of very great injustice. You've been maliciously slandered out of a job, have been abused, or have lost what was most important to you in life and ended up in a situation of utter hopelessness. No human resource or scheme can possibly rectify it. In such cases, you'll need a power that can deliver you from the no-exit corner in which you've been trapped. You'll require an outside intelligence and rescue going far beyond any human resource. No military, political, or high-tech solution will be good enough.

What you need is a Being who creates *ex nihilo*—someone who has the means and ability to manufacture a way out where none exists. You'll need the same God who created the universe out of no preexisting material. He spoke it into existence with just the sheer power of his creative Word. God loves doing this sort of thing for us. He looks for occasions where he can speak into existence what doesn't exist, and he creates exits or entrances that weren't there before, ones we couldn't possibly have anticipated or imagined.

Such experiences of startling coincidences or miraculous rescue, when there was absolutely no hope, are plentifully documented in the annals of church history and modern Christian biography. It is in God, and God alone, where dead things come to life again. It is in the hands of God where power exists to resurrect dead dreams, dead hopes, dead relationships, and eventually, even dead bodies.

What sounds so utterly out of the question to us in our tiny worlds of micro-knowledge is all too easy for God. The words *difficult* or *impossible* don't exist in our Creator's vocabulary. If all this is too hard for you to accept, then maybe it's because the God you've been taught to believe in is too small. Much of our resentment comes from the death of things we value and love. From God's point of view, it can be said clearly and without apology: *There's nothing so alive that it can't die, but there's nothing so dead that it can't be brought back to life.* If this were not true, then there never would have been a New Testament for us to read. Its very origin depended on it. But it's pretty obvious that the historical fact of Jesus's physical resurrection is a very hard thing for many to believe. For some it takes a lifetime of thought, research, and experience to accept it.

God knows how hard it is for our finite, time-bound minds to make room for the eternal and the supernatural.

That's why he grants us aids to help us trust him and believe in the resurrection. This is why we experience life's little resurrections along the way. We call them "rescues" or "reversals" or "God-incidences" created to increase our trust and confidence in him. These deliverances are those *pre-resurrections* that allow us to see with our eyes, hear with our ears, and touch with our fingers the reality of resurrection power.

God creates tailor-made and divinely constructed events of deliverance, healing, unanticipated love, amazing reversals of fortune, unexpected promotions, and unlikely blessings. Second chances, third chances, tenth chances, and so forth are mere *rehearsals* of the final resurrection. It may appear at the moment to be just a chance event, a stroke of good luck, or our own genius. At first, we may not see it for what it is, but when our spiritual eyes start to open, we are overwhelmed by the graciousness and mercy of our God. As we grow in our spiritual and intellectual maturity, we acknowledge the intelligent planning and design that went into it, realizing it had nothing to do with us, but all the praise goes to God.

I began this book with a personal story of how I lost my ability to read for seven very long years, at the worst possible time in my life. I've already described the agonizing struggle that lasted those years and the resentment and confusion that followed.

Now I want to illustrate my point about resurrection by telling you how all this came out in the end. During these years I prayed, stopped praying, and then started praying again after reaching the point of despair—repeatedly. I thought this cycle would never end. But it did. It happened like this.

I had to give up my doctoral studies just one year from completion, leaving the university in Basel, Switzerland, and returning to California, eventually finding work in a church. I couldn't do any other kind of work but could do most of what a pastor needs to do, only with the patience and the help of a wonderful congregation. I recruited a team of willing readers who assisted me, and if there was only one thing my experience taught me, it was dependence upon God and other people.

It was in that caring church I met Shirin, a loving, beautiful, and gifted woman from India, who was the church secretary as well as my secretary. We were married during the Sunday morning worship service, and our reception was the coffee hour following it. (I still think it's the perfect way to get married!) Being my secretary and working closely with me, Shirin was aware of my eye problem. Even so, she was willing to spend her life with me, even if total blindness was my eventual outcome.

Unfortunately, my eyes took a turn for the worse. I had to quit work completely and stay at home. We never spoke of the intensity of this problem to anyone. Our close friends and family had no clue what we were facing. I spent my days with my eyes closed until Shirin came home. She became my eyes. She would read to me, and I would record the main thoughts of an article on my tape recorder. While she was at work, I would listen to the recording and then close my eyes and type my thoughts down. When Shirin returned, she would correct and retype my notes. Not being able to proof what I had typed provided a lot of laughs as we read through my notes, but in this way, I was able to write my first book.

Since we had learned to work so well together, we decided to return to Switzerland, where my eye problem had begun, and take a shot at completing my doctoral degree. The fact that Shirin was able to get a resident permit for Basel was both a miracle and a confirmation that we were following God's leading.

I had completed the written part of my program, but I had to prepare for my oral exam. This was a major challenge. Shirin could read to me the five thousand pages of theology I needed to prepare for the oral exam, but there would come a time when the faculty would place before me texts from the Church Fathers in Latin and Greek that I would have to read, translate, and discuss. She couldn't do that for me. So we hoped and trusted that God just might restore enough of my reading power in time for that event. If he didn't, it would all be for naught, and we would have wasted the year and all our savings. I've never believed that we can somehow force God's hand by our faith, and I was fully prepared to walk away from Basel with nothing in hand, recognizing that God was under no obligation to take away my problem.

It was at this time that God brought an angel into our lives—our Swiss neighbor who lived in the apartment across the hall from us. She was the daughter of missionaries who had left her at home when she was young, while they traveled all over the world "saving souls." The result was that while they were saving others, they had lost their daughter. She hated anything to do with Christian faith, but she loved the people of India, and Shirin became a favorite of hers.

She heard about my eye problem and set up an appointment with a specialist she valued. Shirin knew that I had seen so many specialists by this point and had no intention of going to another one, but our neighbor wasn't one to take no for an answer. It was either go or be dragged there by this strong woman! I met the specialist, Dr. Dominik Wieser, a kind, caring man who took a genuine interest in my condition and told me he was going to do whatever he could to find a solution. A glimmer of hope sprang up in my heart.

Everything was going well. I would attend my lectures

at the university and then twice a week stop by the eye clinic and run through special eye tests and experiments. As months went by, my thesis had been typed, accepted, and stamped, and it was getting closer to the oral exam deadline. Yet there was no breakthrough for my eyes. Now besides being a specialist, Dr. Wieser was also a professor, so when I arrived at the eye clinic he was always accompanied by a number of doctoral students. It seemed that I had become a research project. While he and his students researched, we prayed, our church back home prayed, my parents and friends prayed. But nothing happened. Not a bit of difference. Week after week, everything remained exactly the same, and I was running out of time.

Then one afternoon, in five minutes, only a few weeks from the exam and exactly seven years after the onset of the disorder, everything changed. Dr. Wieser found a pair of old children's glasses in a shoebox and said to me, "Try these." He didn't even know why—it was a shot in the dark since he had tried everything else. Now it was just hit-or-miss.

With those very unique lenses I read for a full five minutes. Five minutes!

You can imagine my euphoria and Dr. Wieser's happiness. We knew that we were on the right track. He worked and reworked the lenses until I built up enough time to face the Church Fathers. I was able to read the texts, finish the oral exam, and graduate in a private ceremony—all in that same morning. To celebrate this tremendous blessing, Shirin and I went straight to a village in the Alps to spend our Christmas there.

I need to add something else to this story. It seems that God, in his providence, had prepared a double portion of his blessing for us that Christmas. Just days after the thrilling and miraculous completion of the oral examination, Shirin and I experienced a rescue from almost certain death. On a long, Christmas Day walk high in the snow-covered Alps, we were so transfixed by the sheer beauty and grandeur of our surroundings that we ended up totally lost and completely alone. In our happy but oblivious wandering, we had drifted off the path and had no idea where we were. Our first thought was, *We're lost in the Swiss Alps on Christmas Day—how romantic! What fun!* But the glitter of it all wore off in a hurry.

When the sun went behind the mountain late in the afternoon, it suddenly became very cold, and we noticed something strange. For the first time there was not a single person we could see near or far in any direction. It was as if the entire mountain had suddenly been abandoned. Where did everyone go? And where were we? What we thought a dream vacation in a winter wonderland was fast becoming a freezing nightmare. The California clothing that was more than sufficient for the sunny day, suddenly was wholly inadequate for the plunging temperatures. *What to do?* We couldn't go back because we didn't know where back was. Going forward was just as bad, since it meant getting even more lost. Our prayers became increasingly more earnest as panic was beginning to set in and we were realizing the seriousness of our situation.

We stopped, thought, and begged God for help. Suddenly we noticed a nearby plateau on the side of the mountain. As we walked toward it, we were stunned by what we saw. Amazingly, unbelievably, there in front of us was a one-horse open sleigh, with the driver sitting motionless on his seat, looking out over the great snowy valley below. We could barely believe our eyes. There was no obvious reason for him to be there. There was nothing but deep snow everywhere around us and not a single person on the mountain or anywhere around it. We just stared in disbelief. Were we hallucinating? The driver didn't seem to be surprised by us and didn't even look to see who was approaching his sleigh. It appeared he was waiting for someone.

Far in the distance, down at the foot of the mountain, was a large resort, so we approached the driver and asked if he could take us there. He nodded but never spoke. We hopped into the sleigh, he covered us with a heavy, colored blanket, and we were off, flying down the side of the mountain in a one-horse open sleigh, on Christmas Day, with sleigh bells ringing loudly and both of us literally laughing all the way. We shouted, "Who would ever believe this!"

Many times since then, Shirin and I have gone over the details of the entire amazing event. *Soli Deo Gloria* (glory to God alone!). That huge "little resurrection" is now part of our family's faith heritage.[4] It is such benefits of God's grace we experience over the years that allow us to get a hold of this resurrection idea. I guess you could say that in the end I was set free from my resentment by God displacing it with mercy and grace. When I entered the long, dark tunnel I had nothing; when I emerged from it years later I had an incredible wife, a doctoral degree, and the experience of a spectacular rescue.

It's these kinds of remarkable, divinely appointed recoveries and happy turnabouts happening in our lives with the passage of time that enable us to have confidence in that final and wonderful resurrection at the end of history.

The resurrection of Jesus, and therefore our future resurrection, tells us that God's last word to us is not death and oblivion, but life—abundant, glorious life. It means that in terms of life's seasons, it doesn't end with winter, but with spring. It isn't the cold, colorless, icy wind of winter that characterizes our final state, but the warm, multi-colored explosion of life on a renewed earth that best depicts our destiny in Jesus Christ. In the language and imagery of Jesus's *signs* (miracles with a message), the Lord saves the best for last (John 2:10).

Jesus's final victory over death delivers us from the overly reverential way in which we treat it: the hushed, almost fearful way we converse when in its presence. Consider the ways we behave and speak in a funeral home with its dark drapes, sadness, and silence. Yet it would be more in keeping with the attitude of Jesus to laugh in the presence of it—in a sense, to laugh in death's face. Truly, this would be the most appropriate of responses to the total victory of Jesus over the ultimate human catastrophe. Of course, it's perfectly natural and normal to grieve over the heartbreaking and devastating loss of loved ones, but we are not to grieve as those who have no hope (1 Thessalonians 4:13). No one else gives us the ability or the right to face up lightheartedly to the deepest, gloomiest pit ever dug for the human race. Death holds no final threat for the follower of the risen Jesus. In the end, we get the last laugh.

Resurrection is much like the lowly caterpillar's transformation into the beautiful and free-flying butterfly. So rather than the aging process signifying the gradual end of vitality and life, it comes to indicate the birth pangs of transformation for real and lasting life. Aging causes us to become more and more uncomfortable with the temporary world in which we live. It makes us increasingly long for the next. It reminds us daily that our permanent home is not this earth, with all its various forms of sorrow, disintegration, pain, and corruption. These will pass away, but the eternal kingdom will never pass away. It serves to focus our attention on the fact that our real abode in a far better world awaits us.

Hope for the Future

We won't be able to get rid of our resentments against God until we come to understand and appreciate fully what it is that he is doing in us and for us. Are we suffering? Are we frustrated at life? Have we lost more than we've won? If so, then you're a perfect candidate for resurrection. No person has ever come to mature faith and strong devotion to the things of God without crossing high mountains, passing through deep valleys, and wandering across a few stretches of barren desert. The biographies of strong Christians and great saints attest to this.

That is just the way life is. Comfort, luxury, prosperity, and ease do not grow us. These are all good things in themselves. They're gifts from our Creator and we should appreciate them. But we have to practice the utmost caution, diligence, and care, as they tend to slow our spiritual growth. Often they lead to pride, independence from God, self-reliance, self-satisfaction, and a casual view toward the things that God loves and wants for us the most. In our humanity, we're prone to be out of tune with God, so we require—*absolutely need*—some force or pressure upon us to bring us back into his orbit. That pressure is adversity. Trials and adversities, even catastrophes of all kinds, are the winds that drive us more quickly toward home. Yes, we hate and dread them, but we can't live well without them.

In the Western world, we believe in what is known popularly as "progress." Progress is the belief that tomorrow will be, or at least *can* be, better than today. It's the hope that drives most people in most places to move from one country to another, to strive for the good life, to go to college, to seek a higher standard of living, and the like. It is perhaps the central doctrine of life in the West and has been embraced by much of the rest of the world. What this view sells us is that human life is getting better all the time, with some sort of nirvana awaiting us in the years ahead.

With this as one of the leading goals of life, we're therefore shocked and confused by anything in this blind faith that disappoints us. When something happens that calls this doctrine into question, we either deny it or come up with dozens of explanations as to why progress is not happening: we don't have enough funding, we need more time for things to develop, we need to try harder to work together, we need more education, and on it goes.

Where did we get the notion that tomorrow holds more promise for us than today? The simple answer: the Bible. In the Old Testament we learn that belief in a better future arose among the ancient Hebrews. It was God's promise that if people followed his will and sought to honor and glorify him on the earth, he would bestow upon them earthly blessings. God spoke his promises to those whom he chose to be a blessing upon the entire earth. In the book of Jeremiah, God declared that even when things seemed as bad as they could be, he had a plan for them that was good (29:11-13). There was light at the end of their long, dark tunnel. God promised to increase their harvests, protect them from their enemies, feed them in times of famine, shelter them in days of pestilence, and lead them to a land of milk and honey. He would create large, happy families for them, prospering them in their business endeavors, and much more. All that he promised them, he would fulfill—as long as they loved him, followed him, and kept his commandments.

The New Testament picks up this same theme and even intensifies the promises with this spectacular addition: following a life of earthly blessings, we'll live in an eternal paradise where righteousness and justice alone dwell. Jesus promises that if we'll seek first the kingdom of God and his righteousness (his perfect will), then the Father will grant us what we need in this life in preparation for the next (see Matthew 6).

So what do we make of the ideal of progress in Western culture, as part of the American dream? It's an idea that originates from the truth of the Bible and its generous God, but the difference is that it operates *without* God. It's all about human effort. It is biblical theology minus the Bible's God. In fact, it is a heresy of Hebrew-Christian ideas.

Shapers of thought and opinion very much like the idea that tomorrow will be better than today, but they don't like the thought that it's the God of the Bible who makes this promise come true. The doctrine of progress is, in reality, having the eggshell without the egg. So when we find ourselves disappointed or unsuccessful in the pursuit of progress, we need to realize that the dream of a better life fades away without God to sustain it. Without the promise-making God who causes the whole thing to work, the notion of life automatically getting better through our sheer efforts becomes the greatest single delusion and superstition of the modern world.

But with God at the center of our hope, a more prosperous and happy future is absolutely the most solid hope and realistic expectation one could ever have. It becomes the most reasonable and intelligent of ideas to hold. If we keep the formula *God + Faith = Solid Hope* intact, then even if we don't realize all the things we hope for on this earth, we still end up with far more than we could ever dream of on our own. Plus, this landslide of blessings will last not just for a quickly passing lifetime but forever.

Keeping the image of our glorious future in front of us, we can exchange for it the losses that cause us to turn away from God and blame him for not answering our prayers today. The ultimate tomorrow, then, the final destiny of all believers, will be the absolute realization of more than we thought and more than we hoped for. If this weren't true, then we wouldn't have a Bible to read in the first place.

People who were direct beneficiaries of God's merciful supply wrote the Bible. They were the people rescued from their enemies, given food when hungry and shelter when cold, and were there to testify that those who put their trust in God through the good times and the bad won't be disappointed. If it's true that the same God who operated in Bible times is still alive, then it follows that he's there to do for us what he did for them. The countless testimonies to this fact are in agreement.

The person who has put his or her trust in the God of the Bible and in Jesus Christ his Son won't be disappointed. If we'll simply wait until the story has a chance to be completed and not bail out early, then we'll see with our own eyes the extravagant provision and elaborate tender mercies of our Creator.

Yet how many of us short-circuit this wonderful denouement of the play and wander off into the thicket of resentment and bitterness that grows on both sides of the pathway? How often we're tempted each day to give it all up, to throw up our hands and walk away from our God in disgust and discouragement. But those who have stayed the course have found that the promises of God's better tomorrows are true. They've testified that they too have heard and been tempted by other voices along the way, but in the end they refused to follow their deceptive lead.

As I've discovered through pastoral counseling, it's much easier to help fallen Christians back on their feet than to help pick up the pieces of a life that has turned away from God. You can be sure that bitterness and disillusionment with life are much greater in the life of someone who denies God. For the believer, there is a ready cure and healthy recovery ahead, but for the other, it's a lot longer and harder journey to healing.

If resentment against God has set in with you for one reason or another, remember that instead of making impetuous judgments or decisions, and instead of laying the blame for your suffering at God's door, try attributing to him the worthiest of motives. Remember the depth of his love for us, his highest regard for our welfare, the greatest level of compassion toward our pain and suffering, and his unwavering determination to bring to pass our best hopes and dreams. Like the prophet Elisha's servant (2 Kings 6:15-17), let's pray that our spiritual eyes may be opened for just an instant to see what's happening behind the scenes of our lives and to see our gracious God's hand in and through it all. Then we can have the hope we need to move forward, to face our future with grace and hope, because God is in control.

Chapter 8

WALKING THE HEALING ROAD

To begin to place God's will at the center of our lives is simple in concept, but not at all easy in practice. It goes against all that we feel inside and all that society tells us. It runs counter to what those around us try to sell us, all that society reminds us of, often by the hour. Advertising, popular wisdom, and even some preaching all reinforce the message that our will is ultimate: "You can't tell someone else what's good or right for them! You need to find your own bliss, what's right for you."

This is the message of our day, but God has a greater word for us: "Come to me, all you who are weary and burdened, and I will give you rest. Take my yoke upon you and learn from me, for I am gentle and humble in heart, and you will find rest for your souls. For my yoke is easy and my burden is light" (Matthew 11:28-30). God always makes a way, and he always has a plan for our lives that will lead us on the ultimate path of healing, even when we are angry at him and doubt his will for us.

We can attempt a lot of healing and restoration work on our own, but unless we turn everything over to him and ask that he lead us on the path from bitterness to joy, we can find ourselves overwhelmed and exhausted by our own efforts. But God, in his graciousness, always makes a way and leads us back to him: "Whether you turn to the right or to the left, your ears will hear a voice behind you, saying, 'This is the way; walk in it' " (Isaiah 30:21).

Keeping Connected

Along the road to healing, we need companions for the journey. Unfortunately, when there is a breach in our relationship with God, one of our instincts is to disconnect ourselves from his people—other believers—because their presence can be a bitter reminder of feeling "betrayed" by the One we trusted completely. We don't want their prayers. We don't care about their encouragements or their advice. We want to be left alone to wallow in our self-pity and disillusionment. It just feels so good to feel so bad, and we don't want anybody messing it up. Besides, when we're in this state of mind, we feel entirely justified in doing whatever we want. We can commit any sin we choose since God doesn't deserve anything from us anyway.

Walking out on God and his people might make us feel good temporarily, but in reality it's walking out on life and hope. We eventually discover that it's much worse on the other side. So, instead of becoming self-absorbed in our own troubles, let's go back to what is real. Remember, our Enemy intends to drive us as quickly and as far as possible from our Creator and Lord. That is his sole occupation, his meat and drink, his obsession. This enemy wants to sever our connections with the people of God. He knows that this connection leads back to God, the main source of healing and life. Don't be manipulated by him into thinking that there's no way back or into falling for the notion that God's existence is merely an adult fairy tale.

If Satan can get us to leave the company of other believers, he can get us where he wants us. Alone and vulnerable, he twists and turns us into any shape he chooses. "Dump the church. It's full of hypocrites anyway!" We can hear his voice telling us in a hundred different ways that the presence of Christians is absolutely the last thing we need.

When full of resentment against God, we don't want to be around people who are filled with love for God and who delight in him. We prefer to be with those who are equally or even more resentful. We take a type of perverted comfort in associating with such persons—those given to finding fault with God and everyone around him. You have probably discovered already that there are plenty of negative people just waiting for you to join them. They appear in your pathway at precisely the right moment, as if it were all somehow carefully planned and timed. (And I believe it is.) Resist this instinct to join them. They are the last ones who can be of any help. What we need are those who have been through the fire themselves and can guide us out of the consuming blaze. Those are the people who can give us some true perspective on what we're facing.

We need the company and knowledge of other Christians (not self-righteous Christians, but honest, sincere believers) because our own personal thin slice of experience can't give us the breadth of perspective we need. It is the believers' family album of life events, not just the solo experience, that puts things in the right framework. The positive things that happen to them—the rescues and restorations—are not just for their personal growth but for ours too.

So that we can be encouraged in our own hopes for rescue, we desperately need to hear how God has led others out of their trials. We need to be near enough to observe how different people came through the fire and how God demonstrated his faithfulness to them in their pain, even though the paths of rescue were invisible to them at the time.

The apostle Paul tells us that the experiences of the

Old Testament believers were written down for us (1 Corinthians 10:11). In the Bible, we can take comfort from
what our ancestors have been through, what happened
to them, and how it all came out in the end. There is
no experience in life that some believer somewhere hasn't
already been through.

For example, let's recall a favorite Old Testament
biography mentioned earlier—the wonderful account of
Joseph (Genesis 37; 39-45). It's packed with useful information and is heavily loaded theologically. It tells us what
happened to one person who trusted God and how, in
the final act of the play, all his tangled problems were
resolved with the most stunning conclusion. But it also
tells of a man who very easily could have, in discouragement and deep resentment, dropped out of the race. He
could have stopped at any one station along the journey
and said, "I've had enough. It's the end. This God just
can't be trusted!"

So many nasty things came his way. Every time he
made one step forward and thought his ship had finally
come in, it was wrecked. He was set back one more time
and then further abused. But we learn from such narra-
tives not to give up too early. We need to follow the story
to the very last moment to get the point. You wouldn't
put a mystery novel down before reading the last chapter,
would you?

But Joseph isn't the only one we can learn from in this respect. There's Moses, David, some of the better kings of Israel and Judah, the prophets Elijah, Elisha, Isaiah, and Jeremiah, and there's Daniel, the determined servant of God held captive in a hostile land, as well as many more up to the present day. We can follow in detail the winding trails of those in different generations, within different cultures and places, who could have become highly resentful of their situations at any point and left the pathway in anger and disgust. The only position from which to view these stories accurately and to be helped by them is from their end—to find out how God rescued and delivered them.

A more recent example is Wilbur Wright, who along with his brother Orville, coinvented powered flight. Wilbur could have had plenty of reasons to resent God. Soon after being convinced that God wanted him to become a preacher of the gospel and making the commitment to obey the call to ministry, he applied and was accepted for theological training. But he never got there. He experienced a sports accident so serious that it disfigured his face.[1]

He was so humiliated by his appearance that he retreated into his father's library to avoid being seen by other people. The question that could have dominated his thinking was, why God would allow this to happen to him just after he had yielded over his entire life to God's service? He could have walked away from God altogether, but through his mother's constant encouragement and prayers, he was able to hang on to his faith in a good and wise God.

Wilbur's dream of flying was sparked by a gift from his father of a rubber-band-powered toy helicopter. Although it was the consensus of scientists that human flight was impossible, he read in the Bible that the word *impossible* is not in God's dictionary (Luke 1:37 ESV). The Wright brothers' vision of the possibility of human flight led to one of the greatest inventions of all time.

Another person I deeply admire is Joni Eareckson Tada. Due to a tragic diving accident in her teens, she ended up a quadriplegic for life. Virtually every conceivable physical ability and pleasure was taken from her. I've tried to imagine what it must have been like to have so much taken away so suddenly and for so long. Yet with the faithfulness of God and by the surprises of his providence, she made so much of what she could do that her gifts and ministry are now known to millions worldwide. The many ways in which she has blessed lives would fill dozens of books. Few preachers or evangelists have had a comparable impact upon the world.

But what lay between her accident as a bright, lively teen and her astounding success today? What kinds of doubts and questions might she have had? If ever there were a case for resenting God for not doing what he could so easily have done, this would be it. With just a word he could have healed her completely. In a split second, with a snap of his fingers, he could have brought her back into perfectly normal life. But this didn't happen. Instead, God chose to set her on a course of lifelong dependence upon him and upon other people. In this dependence, he was to teach her the faith that comes only through long-term suffering and deprivation. Who would be surprised if Tada was filled with the deepest resentment? Yet when you read her writings or hear her speak, you discover something quite different and unexpected. She expresses great love for God and the desire to serve him with whatever capacities she possesses.

Another of my modern-day faith heroes is Nicholas Vujicic, Australian evangelist, motivational speaker, and founder of Life Without Limbs. He says, "I know for certain that God does not make mistakes, but he does make miracles. I am one. You are, too."[2] Vujicic was born with Tetra-amelia syndrome, a rare disorder characterized by the absence of arms and legs. He is one of only seven known survivors of this condition on the planet. Can you imagine what it must be like to have no limbs? The sheer difficulty of doing the thousands of daily actions we take for granted boggles the mind. Vujicic could have given into perpetual despair, blame, and complaint. Instead, he chooses every day to live his life to the honor and glory of God.

While addressing twenty-five thousand people in a soccer stadium in Vietnam, Vujicic asked a young girl who also was born without arms and legs to join him onstage. He said to her, "Do you know why I love God? Because heaven is real. And one day when we get to heaven, we are going to have arms and legs. And we are going to run, and we are going play, and we are going to race."[3]

What produces this kind of joyful faith? Why do some people develop such profound resentments against God for their plight, while others in even worse situations move in the opposite direction? Clearly, the answer lies in the difference between those who find their center in God and those who don't. If we feel that all of life is designed to be for our pleasure and will, then we'll resent whatever frustrates that purpose. However, if we believe that we exist to bring honor and glory to God in the circumstances given us—whatever they are—we'll find out in the proper time how God intends for us to do so.

It's in the experiences of the entire family of faith that we learn this lesson. When we're gathered together, each of us can contribute a piece of the puzzle for everyone's benefit. That is the way it was planned from the beginning. If individually we were sufficient to be all that was needed, there never would have been a people of God in the Old Testament or a church in the New Testament.

We absolutely require the experiences and reports of other believers. For example, I've never seen an angel (as far as I know), but other people I trust implicitly have seen and experienced their help. So I benefit from their encounters. Others say that they've never seen a clear-cut case of a miracle, but I and many others have, so they need our experience to confirm what they read in their Bibles. This is the way it was intended. No one has had enough personal experience or read enough to "have it all," so we desperately need one another to put it all together. Out of the wide, fast-moving river of possible faith events, each of us has only a tiny cupful.

There's an old and familiar analogy describing this: the image of the single coal getting separated from the center of the fire. When together, all the coals stay hot and keep one another from cooling off. But when one gets separated from the rest, it cools off and dies out fairly quickly. This is a relevant illustration of the spiritual life. It's essential that all the coals stay together. When wounded, we mustn't go off by ourselves, like an injured animal attempting some self-healing. It won't work. It never has. God has designed things so that we stay alive and healthy only when we're together.

Yes, of course it's more tempting when deeply hurt by

life to go off in some isolated corner somewhere to grieve quietly or try to patch ourselves up, but this works only to a certain point. More than that, we need to stay in touch with those in the family who can be near enough to encourage us, to share with us how they came through the fire and how God demonstrated his faithfulness to them in their pain, even though it was all completely invisible to them at the time.

I'll say it again: our own personal story isn't enough to get us through. We can't make any final evaluations of God's character or behavior patterns on the basis of the very thin slice of life experiences we acquire, even over an entire lifetime. The atheist thinks he can decide the unimaginably enormous question of God's existence based purely upon the extremely slender amount of evidence he can amass during his one brief life—usually during his first decade or two. We shouldn't think that we're any better off when we try to decide the question of God's reliability on the grounds of what might have happened to us during one short span of months or years.

We need the church. We need the saints. We need their reports that come in day by day and week after week. We can't live the life of faith well and intelligently without the entire family logging in. Just as we need the maps drawn by those who've sailed uncharted waters, we need the vital information of others who've been there in the field (and in the battlefield) with God.

Practicing What Helps You Heal

Ridding our lives of resentment is a journey, and one that we are thankfully not asked to walk alone. This journey requires a recognition of your bitterness and a genuine desire and commitment to stop the downward spiral. It requires a full cooperation of the mind and will. Happily, we have a heavenly Father who is exceedingly compassionate and loves to restore broken relationships. Once we recognize resentment for what it is and have the desire to change, there are some practices we can establish to help along the way.

Honesty

We do ourselves no favors by trying to pretend that things are other than what they are. It gets us nowhere to tell ourselves that since resentment is unspiritual and sinful, it must be some other emotion we're feeling. But the truth is, resentments build up against God whether we acknowledge them or not.

Pretending in the presence of God is one of the silliest things we could ever do. Can we hide truth from our Creator, the essence of truth, who knows our every thought? Is the one who created the ear incapable of hearing, or he who designed the eye unable to see (Psalm 94:9)? It's comical; it's impossible to conceal anything from the only Being in the universe who knows all there is to know. Unless we are totally honest before God about ourselves, we have no hope whatsoever of healing and transformation. Counselor Jade Mazarin writes that she went through an extremely difficult season in her life in which she drew closer to God than she thought possible but was still left with difficult questions and a battle with anger against God:

> But there was another part to me that I was not facing. Beneath the strong assertions that God was wise and good, that He helped me through it all, lay an old hurt I never fully acknowledged. Buried under the "I want to be a good Christian" and "I don't want to feel pain" mantras I was unknowingly clinging to, there was an angry pain that grieved the fact that I even had to go through what I did in the first place....Suddenly, I start talking to God about that suffering years ago. I let myself speak things I never said before:
>
> "Why did I have to go through what I did? Why is it not perfected yet? Was it all really necessary? I trusted you with everything I had! Are you not as great as I thought you were?"
>
> It was painful and emotional. I let myself say whatever came to my mind, from my heart. I also

shared my fears that if He let those things happen before, maybe He could again.

Mazarin points out that simply speaking these words led to a feeling of relief, and a weight being lifted, and maybe it was God himself who led her to speak them. "Therefore," she ends, "let yourself be in touch with whatever you feel toward God. Not even just the anger—which is more like a shield—but the real hurt you feel underneath it. Get in touch with that place. Bringing that place to God. That's the way to start healing."[4]

Gratitude

Any one of us could create a long list of things we want but don't have. But we need to concentrate on what God has given us and be thankful. Why? Because an exercise in gratitude will help change our perspective on our situation and lead us to express our praise to the greatest Giver of gifts. Often our emotions of blame and resentment can trump our intellect by blinding us to God's lavish gifts. In our bitterness, we can no longer see his blessings, even though everyone else around us can.

When we turn to Jesus, place him first, and follow his daily guidance, we will witness his power operating within us. We will gradually leave behind our resentments, self-pity, discontent, and pettiness. In fact, there will come a day when we part ways with all of it. We will finally grasp the greatness of our glorious future and the never-ending grace of God extended toward us. We will move from selfishness to a happy and healthy self-forgetfulness. As only the Holy Spirit can drive out the unholy spirit, so the lion of gratitude will drive away the jackal of resentment.

Have you heard of "positive psychology"? Dr. Sonja Lyubomirsky, author of *The How of Happiness: A Scientific Approach to Getting the Life You Want*, suggests that gratitude:[5]

- helps us savor positive life experiences
- bolsters self-worth and self-esteem
- helps us cope with stress and trauma
- encourages moral behavior
- strengthens relationships
- inhibits comparing with others
- diminishes negative emotions
- keeps us from taking joys for granted and thus extends our joy

New studies now focus on enhancing mental health, not just treating mental illness: "Lyubomirsky's research demonstrates that expressing gratitude has several benefits. People who are grateful are likely to be happier, hopeful and energetic, and they possess positive emotions more frequently. Individuals also tend to be more spiritual or religious, forgiving, empathetic and helpful, while being less depressed, envious or neurotic."[6]

Bottom line? Be thankful! Sincere thankfulness is a powerful antidote to resentments and hostilities of every kind. It works wonders on the human level. Just look at the surly waiter or grumpy taxi driver who receives a bigger tip than expected. Observe the criticized and harassed teacher who is thanked and praised by the parent at the end of the school year. Watch and see how someone's spirit opens up like a flower in the sun when genuine appreciation is expressed.

Our thankfulness toward God deepens and widens as we take off the blinders and open our eyes to all he has given. Gratitude and resentment are in a teeter-totter relationship to each other; the more one grows, the more the other shrinks. Throughout the Bible, we are encouraged to praise God and give thanks to him. As a rule, you can't praise God and resent him at the same time. Being grateful is a key component of a Christian's life. This is one of those aspects of our life that will increase joy and contentment with everything around us.

Try this: find yourself a nice quiet corner or "me place," a cup of espresso or tea, and a notebook. Then start listing every single reason to be thankful. Remember one by one all the events that suggest a rescue, an unexpected blessing, a positive reversal, or some intervention of God. Start with your very first memories in life. Count everything that could be regarded as a gift that may have slipped your memory.

Once you've started your Notebook of Praise and Thanks, add to it each day, finding one more thing to be thankful for. And don't stop there. Start flooding your surroundings with positive messages—encouraging Bible verses on refrigerator magnets or calendars, beautiful pictures, connecting with happy people, those that encourage you to reach for your lost dreams, or those who refill your empty optimism tank.

Forgiveness

Tied closely to gratitude is forgiveness. When we learn to forgive, we attain higher levels of personal satisfaction and delight. A by-product is that happier people have been found to live longer, more productive lives. This leads to more optimism and joy. I believe that Dr. Sonja Lyubomirsky's concrete results validate the Christian claim that God created us to be people of joy—a clear connection between being believers and having more stress-free lives.

Forgive those who have (or you think have) hurt you. If possible, go to the person and try to mend the relationship. But keep in mind that forgiving other people can be a tricky business. Maybe they don't want your forgiveness or don't think they've done anything to need it. There is a popular school of thought among Christians today that bypasses the age-old process of confession and forgiveness. We are now often encouraged to say to the offender, "You really hurt me when you did/said (fill in the blank), but I want you to know that I forgive you." But if there is obviously no interest in being forgiven, unless it is a gift given freely and received joyfully, this is a complete waste of time. Worse, it's absolutely meaningless. We have no right or obligation to offer someone the priceless gift of forgiveness unless there is some desire or request for it. Let's not dump on others something unwanted or hand out free passes that have no value and are of no cost to anyone.

Here's what I mean: the act of Christian forgiveness is a profound spiritual transaction that is based upon God's gracious act toward us. Willing forgiveness follows unforced and unmanipulated confession. The New Testament puts it like this: "If we confess our sins, he is faithful and just and will forgive us our sins and purify us from all unrighteousness" (1 John 1:9). Jesus taught that we are to forgive others as many times as it is asked for (Luke 17:3-4).

To try to forgive on our own terms with some sort of cheap, fast-food forgiveness is to short-circuit this life-changing event of grace, leaving the offender unrepentant, unchanged, and therefore un-forgiven. So we clear the decks within our own hearts, prepared to forgive and reconcile the moment it is asked for. And if it never is asked for, the burden is lifted from us and remains on them.

Human relationships are complex, but when it comes to forgiveness, it is far different and much simpler with God. We have a heavenly Father whose compassion exceeds all boundaries and human reason and who can't wait to forgive our sins and restore our fellowship with him. Unlike us humans, he holds no grudges and quickly sends our guilt to the farthest point of the horizon (Psalm 103:8-12).

Feeding the Mind and Soul

Take some intentional time to nurture yourself. Maybe even learn to laugh out loud! Laughter therapy (also known as humor therapy) is seeing huge benefits for patients these days. The Cancer Treatment Centers of America even have a page on their website dedicated to encouraging their patients to laugh. Here's what they say:

> For years, the use of humor has been used in medicine. Surgeons used humor to distract patients from pain as early as the 13th century. Later, in the 20th century, came the scientific study of the effect of humor on physical wellness. Many credit this to Norman Cousins. After years of prolonged pain from

a serious illness, Cousins claims to have cured himself
with a self-invented regimen of laughter and vitamins.
In his 1979 book *Anatomy of an Illness*, Cousins
describes how watching comedic movies helped him
recover.[7,8]

So see funny movies or shows or movies that cheer or
inspire you. Laughter is one of the most simple and
cost-effective ways to release stress and start us on the
road to healing.

Take the time to saturate yourself with the beauty
of nature, God's creation. Praise him for each thing you
see that he has made. Spend more time outdoors. Walk
through meadows and forests with your family, friends, or
pets. Put down Facebook and discover more ways to serve
others. Spend less time fixated on the media and its constant flow of bad news of every kind. Did you know that it
usually takes a number of positive thoughts to counter the
effects of even one negative message? Protect your mind.

Do what you can to consciously rid yourself of exter-
nal negative influences as well as your own negative internal dialogue. God created you in his image—a unique and
brilliant designer. Don't let what you *think* you see in the
mirror (or what negative things others are saying about
you) bring you down. You were designed with a purpose
tailor-made for you. No one else can take your place.

Get involved in helping other people in need, animal

rescue work, or anything that directs your attention outside yourself. God has so arranged the human heart to be fulfilled not by exclusively seeking its own desires and welfare but rather by seeking his will and the welfare of our neighbor. When you build into your life this discipline of praise and thanksgiving and give yourself away to others—helping, serving, and nurturing—you'll soon discover that you don't have time for resentment. You'll find your anger fading and you'll start to become the person God created you to be—loving, generous, and more joyful.

Will you be happy all the time? There's nothing in the scriptures to indicate that we are to be deliriously happy every minute of the day. However, in time (God's time) you'll grow more confident and joyful and have the strength to overcome the problems that come your way. You'll possess a peace and contentment—a peace that passes all understanding and one that comes only through having the Spirit of Jesus dwelling and reigning in you. Remember the apostle Paul, who was more in tune with the Holy Spirit than most of us, still had his excruciating experiences of suffering and confusion. We can say with him:

> We are hard pressed on every side, but not crushed; perplexed, but not in despair; persecuted, but not abandoned; struck down, but not destroyed. We

always carry around in our body the death of Jesus,
so that the life of Jesus may also be revealed in our
body. For we who are alive are always being given
over to death for Jesus' sake, so that his life may be
revealed in our mortal body. (2 Corinthians 4:8-11)

When we claim this promise, our losses, grief, and
sorrows will no longer be the things that define us but
will be subordinated to a life subject to God's sovereignty
and blessing. In this straightforward, uncomplicated plan
lies our prescription for wholeness and joy. In, with, and
by Jesus Christ, we can do all things!

Let God Be the Ultimate Healer

I didn't write this book as a handy self-help book,
because ultimately, there is no self-help here. If resentment has left us in a place of broken fellowship with God,
yes, there are things we can do, but we still need a miracle. God has to do something for us.

In the same way that God sought us out and took the
initiative in creating our relationship with him and his
Son (John 6:44), he preserves us to the very last day (Jude
24, 25). These are things that only God can do. See the
wilderness of resentment as being on a sinking ship. In
such circumstances, what we need is not primarily good
advice or a nice set of theological doctrines but a someone who has the power and the means to rush to our

rescue. When we are drowning in resentment, God can rescue us, and he will.

We have a tender-hearted God who is not unsympathetic toward us and is not unaware of all our temptations, even our temptations to blame and resent him. If Jesus is the Savior who brings us into redemption while we are still dead in our sins and hostile to him (Romans 5:6-11), he is also the Good Shepherd who leaves the flock to search out and bring back the one wandering sheep. It's very likely he'll have to do this more than once in our lifetime, for we all tend to wander off the path of life. We can't seem to help ourselves.

The message of God's stubborn faithfulness and determination to save and to keep what he first pursued is found throughout both the Old and New testaments. Isaiah 49:14-16 says:

> But Zion said, "The LORD has forsaken me,
>   the Lord has forgotten me."
> "Can a mother forget the baby at her breast
>   and have no compassion on the child she has
>   borne?
> Though she may forget,
>   I will not forget you!
> See, I have engraved you on the palms of my
> hands;
>   your walls are ever before me."

What a wonderful image of God to fix in our minds! Have you watched the great delight a mother takes in her infant? She is utterly focused on the tiny life so dependent upon her and would do everything in her power to keep and protect it from any threat. And if the child later rejects the mother, she spends the rest of her life longing for a loving reunion. Even at this responsibility, humans can fail, but not so with God. When the last mother has forgotten her child, God is still just as focused and fixed on our welfare.

Further, the apostle Paul assures us in Romans 8:38-39 that nothing—absolutely nothing—will ever be able to take away God's love for us: "For I am convinced that neither death nor life, neither angels nor demons, neither the present nor the future, nor any powers, neither height nor depth, nor anything else in all creation, will be able to separate us from the love of God that is in Christ Jesus our Lord."

God's everlasting love and faithfulness—his kindnesses toward me in my journey from resentment to joy, fulfillment, and gratitude—have dumbfounded me. When I thought that he had every reason to turn his back on me, he didn't. When I assumed he had abandoned me and wasn't paying attention to my cries for help, I later discovered unbelievable answers to my prayers.

Why did God come to rescue me when I was adrift from him? Didn't I have to get better and straighten out my life before I could come back to a normal relationship with him? I discovered if that were true, none of us would ever be believers.

In my journey toward restoration with my loving Father, I learned a whole lot more. When we get rid of resentment and turn toward our Creator, we will find life opening up to us in ways that we never thought possible. I am proof of this—the bitterness is gone. Vanished. This has made it possible for me to be aware of God's plans and to live with thankfulness for all the good things he has brought to me, for all the times my prayers have been answered with an extravagant yes or a life-saving no. Put simply, God has blessed me out of my resentment.

Anne Peterson, poet and author of *Broken: A Story of Abuse, Survival, and Hope*, had plenty of reasons to resent God, being called upon to experience more profound tragedies and losses in life than most. From anger to resentment to full-blown bitterness, Anne was mad at God and let him know it. And then, she discovered a profound truth so many of us have discovered. Reflect on the words of her poem:

How Dare You, God
I stood before an empty sky
and shook my fist clenched tight,
I opened up my very soul,
and screamed with all my might,

How dare you, God, how dare you
take everything of mine.
While others all around me
seem so carefree most the time.

I've watched my loved ones disappear
from my family,
and I can't take it anymore,
so get away from me!

With silence all around me,
I wait for Him to leave
like others who have disappeared
when I would start to grieve.

I feel his arms encircle me,
and hear Him gently say,
"I know that you're upset with me,
but I am here to stay."[9]

No matter where we go or what we do, God promises to be our Helper and our Guide. In short, then, the
life of Christian discipleship means this: *God is in charge.
He sets the course, makes all the necessary course corrections, and brings us safely to our destination.*

My own story had a wonderful ending. God brought
healing to my eyes to the point that I can watch movies,
travel the world, have dinners with family and friends,
read, write, study, and all the things I missed for so many

years. I went from sitting in a dark room to living a wild, Technicolor life of gratitude and joy. I travel around Europe with my wife, watch my daughters' concerts with their rock band, and am able to minister to wonderful congregations. And the more I let go of my resentment over those lost years, the more fulfilled and happy my life became.

No, life hasn't been a total joyride since those days, but I learned something from them. My time of resentment and release from it was the boot camp that prepared me to face new challenges and perils (and losses) along the way. I learned that if the tide of faith can go out, it can come back in.

God tells us that he has our name tattooed on the palm of his hand where it can't possibly be forgotten (Isaiah 49:16). He is ever mindful of us and our needs. Jesus reiterates this truth when he says that he will be with us to the end (Matthew 28:20). He said this to those disciples closest to him, who did leave and forsake him, and he says it to us.

God is, and always will be, the waiting father of Jesus's parable, who allows the wandering child to venture far from home but waits eagerly for his or her return. No one has ever regretted coming home from the far country, so don't waste a single minute more away from our loving Father.

You can discover what many others have already found, that whatever drove you away in the first place is nothing more than a complete misperception of everything that is real. Don't walk; run to him! Let him enfold you into his arms. There's no better time than right now. You'll have the rest of your life to discover how true these old words of Jeremiah are for you today:

> The Lord appeared to him from far away.
> I have loved you with an everlasting love;
>   therefore I have continued my faithfulness to
>   you. (Jeremiah 31:3 ESV)

The fulfillment of our dreams and hopes lies not in angrily thrusting God out of our lives and marching ahead with our own plans but in putting Jesus first. It is in experiencing his loving-kindness and grace toward us that we find the way out and the way in—*out* of the spiral of resentment and bitterness, and *in* to the life of joy, meaning, and fulfillment we were looking for all along.

ACKNOWLEDGMENTS

My heartfelt thanks to my wife, Shirin, and daughters, Sarah and Stephanie, for their encouragement and help on this manuscript; to Anne Peterson for permission to use her inspiring poem, "How Dare You, God"; to my hard-working agent, Cyle Young; and to Carl Spiva and Twyla Lunn for reading the manuscript in its earliest forms and for their many encouraging remarks. Thank you to those of you who were brave enough to step forward and share your honest feelings of anger, hurt, disappointment, and bitterness toward God, a subject that is, unfortunately, still taboo in our Christian circles. It's my prayer that this book will help change this and bring healing to others trapped in this dark and frustrating valley.

NOTES

Introduction

1. "Charles Spurgeon's 'Morning and Evening'—February 22, Evening," *Theology Mix*, February 22, 2018, https://theologymix.com/spurgeon-audio-podcast/charles-spurgeons-morning-and-evening-february-22-evening.

1. When Anger Turns Upward

1. Carrie Fisher, *The Best Awful: A Novel by Carrie Fisher* (New York: Simon and Schuster, 2003), 30.

2. Elizabeth Landau, "Anger at God Common, Even Among Atheists," CNN, January 1, 2011, http://thechart.blogs.cnn.com/2011/01/01/anger-at-god-common-even-among-atheists.

3. Robert C. Loveless (author) and Wendell P. Loveless (composer), "Every Day with Jesus" (1936), Hymnary.org, https://hymnary.org/hymn/RH2011/254.

2. When Life Is Disappointing

1. Paul J. Pastor, "How to Pray When You're Pissed at God," *Christianity Today*, July 2013, www.christianitytoday.com/pastors/2013/july-online-only/how-to-pray-when-youre-pissed-at-god.html.

3. When We Aren't Sure What to Make of God—and Other Believers

1. "World Watch List," *Open Doors USA*, www.opendoors usa.org/christian-persecution/world-watch-list.

2. Hollie McKay, "North Korea: How Christians Survive in the World's Most Anti-Christian Nation," August 19, 2017, *Fox News*, www.foxnews.com/world/2017/08/18/north-korea -how-christians-survive-in-worlds-most-anti-christian-nation .html.

3. McKay, "North Korea."

4. Soon Ok Lee, *Eyes of the Tailless Animals: Prison Memoirs of a North Korean Woman* (Bartlesville, OK: Living Sacrifice Book Co., 1999).

5. Confucius, *The Analects* [c. 500 BCE] (London: Penguin Classics, 1998), XV:24. Ancient Greek philosopher Thales wrote, "Avoid doing what you would blame others for doing" (Diogenes Laërtius, *The Lives and Opinions of Eminent Philosophers* [New York: Oia Press, 2015]).

6. Jacob Bailey Moore Pamphlet Collection, *January 1821*, vol. 3 of *The Christian Spectator* (London: Forgotten Books, 2017), 186.

7. Cyril C. Richardson, *Early Christian Fathers* (New York: The Macmillan Company, 1970), 217.

4. Resentment's Legacy

1. Theodore Dalrymple, "The Uses of Resentment," *Psychology Today*, March–April 1995, www.psychologytoday .com/articles/199503/the-uses-resentment.

2. Dalrymple, "Uses of Resentment."

3. Paul C. Vitz, *Faith of the Fatherless: The Psychology of Atheism* (San Francisco: Ignatius Press, 2013). See also Paul C. Vitz and J. Garner, "Christianity and Psychoanalysis, Part 1: Jesus as the Anti-Oedipus," *Journal of Psychology and Theology* 12, no. 1 (1984): 4–14; and Paul C. Vitz and

J. Garner, "Christianity and Psychoanalysis, Part 2: Jesus as the Anti-Oedipus," *Journal of Psychology and Theology* 12, no. 2 (1984): 82–89.

4. Mortimer J. Adler, *Philosopher at Large: An Intellectual Autobiography* (New York: Macmillan, 1977).

5. In my view, the best work on this subject is ACLU attorney and constitutional scholar Robert L. Cord's *Separation of Church and State: Historical Fact and Current Fiction* (Grand Rapids: Baker, 1988).

5. A Correct View of God

1. John Newton, "Amazing Grace," *Olney Hymns*, 1779.

2. Peter Wagner, "The Awesome Argentina Revival," *Journal of Aggressive Christianity* 26 (August–September 2003).

3. Howard L. Malone (LTC), "A Christian Soldier's Perspective on Afghanistan," *The Spoken Word Church*, http://thespokenwordchurch.org/bible-study-tools-2/articles/a-christian-soldiers-perspective-on-afghanistan.

4. "Charles Spurgeon's 'Morning and Evening'—November 12, Morning," *Theology Mix*, November 12, 2017, https://theologymix.com/spurgeon-audio-podcast/charles-spurgeons-morning-and-evening-november-12-morning.

5. Hudson Taylor, *The Autobiography of Hudson Taylor: Missionary to China* (Louisville: GLH, 2011), Kindle edition, 52–56.

6. The Importance of Good Teaching

1. Tad Friend, "Jumpers: The Fatal Grandeur of the Golden Gate Bridge," *The New Yorker*, October 13, 2003, www.newyorker.com/magazine/2003/10/13/jumpers.

2. Westminster Shorter Catechism, Center for Reformed Theology and Apologetics, www.reformed.org/documents/wsc/index.html?_top=http://www.reformed.org/documents/WSC.html.

3. Isaac Watts, "Alas! and Did My Savior Bleed," 1707, Timeless Truths Free Online Library, https://library.timelesstruths.org/music/Alas_and_Did_My_Savior_Bleed/.

4. Cyril C. Richardson, *Early Christian Fathers* (New York: Touchstone, 1995).

7. Living in a Redemption Story

1. Johann Franck, "Jesus, Priceless Treasure," trans. Catherine Winkworth, *The United Methodist Hymnal* (Nashville: The United Methodist Publishing House, 1989), 532.

2. "Global Anti-Aging Market Size & Trends Will Reach $216.52 Billion by 2021: Zion Market Research," *Zion Market Research*, June 5, 2017, https://globenewswire.com/news-release/2017/06/05/1007965/0/en/Global-Anti-Aging-Market-Size-Trends-Will-Reach-216-52-Billion-by-2021-Zion-Market-Research.html.

3. See C. S. Lewis, *The Abolition of Man* (San Francisco: HarperOne, 2015). Also, visit your nearest university library and look into the massive work *The Encyclopedia of Religion and Ethics*, edited by James Hastings (Edinburgh: T&T Clark, 1908).

4. I wrote about this story in my article "James Bond and the Impossible Christmas" on *Theology Mix*, December 25, 2017, https://theologymix.com/holidays/james-bond-and-the-impossible-christmas.

8. Walking the Healing Road

1. Charles Ludwig, *The Wright Brothers: They Gave Us Wings*, Sowers World Heroes Series (Milford, MI: Mott Media, 1985).

2. Keith Maginn, *(Extra)Ordinary: More Inspirational Stories of Everyday People.* (Georgetown, OH: KiCam Projects, 2017).

3. Associated Press, "Part Evangelist, Part Motivational

Speaker, Australian Man Born Without Arms and Legs Takes Gospel to Unlikely Places," *National Post*, May, 25, 2013, http://nationalpost.com/holy-post/part-evangelist-part-motivational-speaker-australian-man-born-without-arms-and-legs-takes-message-to-unlikely-places.

4. Jade Mazarin, "When It's Good to Get Angry with God," *Relevant Magazine*, January 13, 2015, https://relevantmagazine.com/god/practical-faith/when-its-good-get-angry-god.

5. Sonja Lyubomirsky, *The How of Happiness: A New Approach to Getting the Life You Want* (New York: Penguin Books, 2008).

6. Lauren Suval, "The Relationship Between Happiness and Gratitude," *Psych Central* blog post, August 9, 2012, https://psychcentral.com/blog/the-relationship-between-happiness-and-gratitude.

7. "Laughter Therapy," Cancer Treatment Centers of America, www.cancercenter.com/treatments/laughter-therapy.

8. Norman Cousins, *Anatomy of an Illness: As Perceived by the Patient*, Twentieth Anniversary Edition (New York: W. W. Norton & Company, 2005).

9. Anne Peterson, *Broken: A Story of Abuse, Survival, and Hope* (n.p., 2013). Poem reprinted with author's permission.

ABOUT THE AUTHOR

As an ordained Presbyterian pastor, Dr. John I. Snyder has served congregations in the United States and Europe and has planted churches in California and Switzerland. He is the lead author, advisor, and regular contributor for theology and culture blog *Theology Mix* and has been a guest on *Christian Devotion Speak Up* and podcasts *Ordinary Pastors* and *After the Sermon*.

Snyder is the author of *Your 100 Day Prayer* and a contributor to *Theology Today, Dialog, Theologische Zeitschrift, Journal of the Evangelical Theological Society, The Washington Times*, and others. He has also appeared on Fox News, Focus the Family, and Insight with Paul Arthur on Miracle TV.

He received his master of theology and master of divinity degrees from Princeton Theological Seminary and his doctor of theology degree in New Testament Studies from the University of Basel, Switzerland.

He and his wife, Shirin, and their daughters Sarah and Stephanie share their time between California and Europe.